3rd Edition

HOW TO PLAY THE

5-STRING BANJO

a manual for beginners

by Peter Seeger

Published By Homespun Music Instruction   *Woodstock, NY 12498*

ISBN-13 : 978-1-59773-164-5

Preface to second edition, 1954

This is the second edition of this manual. It has been added to and revised slightly, and thereby, it is hoped, improved. The first edition was mimeographed, its stencils having been typed in a variety of hotel rooms while the author was accompanying Henry Wallace in the presidential campaign of 1948. The first printing of 100 copies sold out in three years. The second printing, also mimeographed, sold its 500 copies in another three years. A casual statistician might thus deduce (assuming the same rate of increase continues,) that 390,000 copies will be sold within the next twelve years. As G. B. Shaw said, however, 'there are lies, damned lies, and statistics'. The author prudently limits this printing to 3000.

To go with this manual, a Long Playing record has been prepared in which one can hear all important examples in this book played two ways: very slowly and clearly, and up to tempo. This should be of special value to those who cannot read music, or have no banjo playing friends or teachers to help them over the hurdles. The record costs $6.98 and can be ordered from Folkways Records, 43 West 61st St., N.Y., N.Y. 10023.

The first edition said "Copyright 1948". This we fear, was a falsehood. The necessary four bucks were never shelled out. Furthermore, upon reflection, and with the good example of J. Frank Dobie of Texas, it is not copyright in 1954. Permission is hereby given to reprint, whenever needed.

Special acknowledgement and thanks go to Fleming Brown, artist and banjo picker of Chicago, and to Edward Epstein, likewise, of New York City, for their fine pen and ink drawings.

Thanks also to Marty Cohen, the banjo engineer, for assistance in plans for lengthening banjo necks. Also to Woody Wachtel, Dave Sear, Joe Jaffee, and Jerry Silverman, for advice and suggestions. To Lillian Goodman for her typing. To Margot Mayo and to Harry West for use of their photographs of Rufus Crisp, Samantha Bumgarner, and Uncle Dave Macon. To Tony Schwartz for cover and title page.

Thanks most of all to Toshi-Aline Seeger for paste-up and layout, and general patience, perseverance, and perspicacity.

* * * * * *

Dedicated with thanks to the many men and women, in the many walks of life, who helped me learn the banjo, and to those whose records I listened to, such as Uncle Dave Macon, Rufus Crisp, Samantha Bumgarner, Bascom Lunsford, Lilly Mae Ledford and Earl Scruggs.

Dedicated also to the men and women who, still earlier, taught them.

Dedicated to the folks who will learn from us, carrying an age-old tradition on. Around and around this old world, ring, ring the banjo.

Printed in the United States of America

Painting of Henry Alexander by Corydon Bell

Preface to third edition, 1961

Since this manual was first published, a small musical revolution has taken place in the USA. The revival of interest in folk music has spread widely, and along with it, the 5-string banjo really has made a comeback - often due to the music of the young people who bought copies of this book.

At the same time, without the help of this or any book, thousands have used the old folk method of Listen - Watch - and Try, to teach themselves the sparkling banjo styles of such musicians as Earl Scruggs, Ralph Stanley, and other bluegrass banjo pickers. (See page 38).

In this third edition I have tried to repair some of the numerous typographical errors in the earlier editions. Nearly every chapter has been enlarged, and the appendix has been brought up to date, in order to mention some of the other banjo books available now, such as ones by my sister Peggy, and by Billy Faier. Unfortunately, since the book is now seventy-two pages instead of forty, the price had to go up too.

The book being bigger also, unfortunately, increases the greatest danger: that the beginner will try to learn it all at once. This is the surest recipe for failure. As Scruggs himself writes, "A good point to remember is, do not try to learn too much at one time. If it is only making a few chords, do that over and over until you can do that with very little effort." With this book, leaf through it quickly, light on to the chapter you are most interested in, and don't feel a bit badly about ignoring the rest. Don't be like the hungry boy in the cafeteria who loaded his tray with far more than he could eat.

Lastly, let me thank many friends for criticisms and suggestions. Especial thanks to members of my family, Toshi, Danny, and Mika, who helped with typing and paste-up. Old grandpa is going out on the porch and pick a banjo himself for a while, and watch the evening sun.

The following songs on page 25 and 26 are printed by permission:
"Streets of Laredo" from Cowboy Songs, by John A. Lomax. "Brandy Leave Me Alone" English words © by Joseph Marais. "Tee Roo" collected from the singing of the Gant family by John A. and Alan Lomax. "The Strangest Dream" words and music by Ed McCurdy. "Irene Goodnight" collected from the singing of Huddie Ledbetter by John A. and Alan Lomax © Ludlow Music. "The Frozen Logger" by James Stephenson, "So Long, It's been good to know you" by Woody Guthrie. ©1950 and 1951 by Folkways Music, Inc.

Samantha Bumgarner

TABLE OF CONTENTS

I

HISTORY

Played by hundreds of thousands of Americans 75 or 100 years ago, by 1940 this instrument had nearly died out.

Negro slaves brought the first banjoes over here; before that the origin is disputed. Possibly the Arabs brought it to the African west coast; possibly the Arabs themselves picked it up from civilizations further east. At any rate, 125 years ago the banjo consisted basically of three strings, with maybe just a possum hide stretched across a gourd, for a drum.

Then began a period of experimentation. Frets were added, various numbers of strings tried out, and one Joe Sweeney of Virginia was credited with inventing in 1831 a little fifth string running from a little peg halfway up the neck. ✳✳

It was this version that became fantastically popular and was picked up by the country as a whole. It travelled west in the covered wagons, and one could be found hanging on the wall of any farmhouse or mining shack. Even trained singers, such as Patti, would play one for amusement. Later, concert virtuosos, with phenomenal techniques, tried to take it out of the domain of the minstrel shows ...... I've even heard of the William Tell overture being attempted on a banjo.

With the advent of ragtime and jazz, around the turn of the Century, the long necked 5-stringer was gradually abandoned in favor of the shorter Tenor Banjo. This was tuned differently, and with heavier strings, to better compete with the loud brass instruments. The Tenor Banjo had its hey-day in the 1920's, and then in turn was left behind by modern dance bands.

For many years the 5-string banjo was almost forgotten; instrument companies stopped making them; a hock shop was the most likely place to find one. Still, it was played by back-country people, especially in the South to accompany ballads and play for square dances. And precisely because it is so excellently suited for such work, the old 5-stringer is now making a comeback.

THIS MANUAL......

....will not make a virtuoso out of anyone, but I have compressed into its few pages almost everything I know about playing the banjo.✳With its help you can teach yourself to accompany many songs. And it will take you considerably shorter time than it took me. I picked up the instrument from many different people, in travelling through the country.

THE BANJO LESSON   by Henry Tanner

I would suggest that you leaf through this entire manual first, to see what its scope is. Beginners may have to ignore whole chunks; someone who already knows the rudiments of music can skip other parts if he likes. (Few would want to learn it all.)

It may take you anywhere from a few months to a few years to work your way through, depending on how good an ear you have; how quickly your fingers can coordinate, and how continuously you play.

Get together with others who like to sing, and try running through the various folksongs, ballads, blues, and dance tunes I have given as examples. Don't think of yourself as "practicing" in the formal sense, but simply keep on playing a lot. As with tap-dancing, this banjo technique is nothing more than doing a few simple things over and over, till the whole procedure is fast and relaxed.

Folk tunes are used throughout as examples, to teach the instrument. I feel the banjo is most suited to them. However, I may be prejudiced - probably am - therefore please feel free to experiment.

This manual cannot itself teach you to play the banjo. It can, however, I hope, help you to teach yourself.

✳✳ For more historical data see Appendix 5
✳ ....and some I don't know.

II

A BASIC STRUM

1) If you have never before played a banjo, check Appendix #1 to see how to take care of the instrument, and to learn the names of its various parts.

2) Tune up your banjo as follows:

5th string (the one running from the peg half way up the neck). .G (4 notes (a "fifth") above middle C)

4th string (the one next to the 5th). . . . . C (one octave below middle C)

3rd (next to the 4th) . . . . G (3 notes (a "fourth") below middle C)

2nd (next to 3rd). . . . . . B (one note below middle C)

1st. . . . . D (one note above middle C)

You can get a banjo in relative good tune with itself by the following method:
a) Tune the 4th string to approximately the right tension, with your ear, if there is nothing else to help you.
b) Fret this 4th string at the 7th fret, as shown at right. Tune the 3rd string to the exact same pitch (unison).
c) Fret the 3rd string at the 4th fret, and tune the 2nd string to the same pitch.
d) Fret the 2nd string at the 3rd fret, and tune the 1st string to unison with it.
e) Fret the 1st string at the 5th fret, and tune the 5th string to the same pitch.
Assuming that you have a good banjo, with frets and strings and bridge in proper order, the banjo should be in fairly good tune. If the 4th string was a little low or high to begin with, all the other strings will likewise be low or high.

Easier yet is to use a pitchpipe or a piano.

Middle C

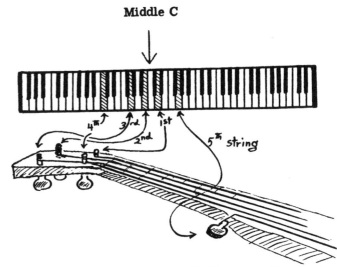

The above is the standard "C" tuning; there are other tunings you will learn later on.

3) Sit and hold the banjo somewhat in the manner shown at right. Keep the face of the drum vertical, the other end about level with your left shoulder. (Later you can fasten a strap to your brackets and play standing up, but it's easier to learn sitting down.)

4) With your left hand make the following "chord". Your fingers should come down where the dots are, not directly on the fret, but "slightly south" of them. Do not let your fingertip touch more than one string now; press down firmly to get a clear tone.

Make sure the fingernails of your left hand are very short, so that they do not hinder your fingers from fretting the strings firmly and cleanly. (See Appendix 5 about this).

5) With your right hand do as follows: the index finger should pluck up, sounding the 1st string only. Then with the other three fingers (ignore the thumb for the moment) brush down across all five strings. Use the whole wrist, so it's not just a finger motion.

Try doing this regularly in march time: up, down, up down; one, two, one, two. This is the basic strum.

The notes you are playing would look like this on music paper.

The letter "I" stands for the index finger of the right hand plucking up.

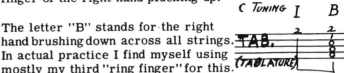

The letter "B" stands for the right hand brushing down across all strings. In actual practice I find myself using mostly my third "ring finger" for this. Other banjo players tend to use mostly the fingernail of their middle finger, or their index finger, as they brush down and across the strings. . You will have to experiment for yourself, and decide which effect you prefer. In any case, the whole wrist turns, not just the finger.

HOW TO READ TABLATURE:

The lower set of five horizontal lines does not represent a music staff. They are the five strings of the banjo. When a number is placed on a certain line, it means that string is sounded in some way, and the number represents the fret at which the left hand stops the string. Tablature was a system of music writing used by lute players in 16th Century Europe. This is a simplified version. If you cannot read music, you can still puzzle your way through this manual by reading the tablature.

Here's how. If your hand were to make a C chord, thus:  Tablature would describe it thus:

And if you wanted to play a scale (do, re, mi, fa, sol, la, ti, do) starting on the 4th string, and plucking each note with the index finger of the right hand, tablature would show it thus:

6) With your left hand learn two more chords now:

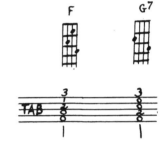

Tablature would describe them this way:

7) Knowing three chords, your way is now clear to accompany simple songs in the key of C. Don't bother learning any other chords as yet. Concentrate on getting a good easy rhythm out of your right hand. The following song I have written out. If you do not know how to read music yet (see Appendix IV) skip over this and don't spend too much time trying to puzzle it out. You'll find it a help to start learning, however, especially if you are studying this manual without the help of a teacher.

THE UNION WAY

Position of left hand and name of chord being used:

Melody being sung by the voice:

Words of song:

Notes being played by the banjo:

How the strings are sounded:

Tablature to locate correct string and correct fret ("O" stands for an open, unfretted string).

7

You can figure out the accompaniment yourself to the rest of the first verse of "The Union Way".

```
    C                         F
    But since our plant got organized
    G7                        C
    We're living much more civilized.
```

(Complete song, words by Ray Glaser, can be found in "The People's Songbook". Same tune as "Little Brown Jug".)

You'll note that throughout this manual I often neglect to write down any notes for the 4th string, the bass string, to play.

I've done this partly because in actual practice it is rarely sounded directly when the fingernails brush across the strings. Cluttering up the music staves and tablature with big four and five note chords actually would look misleading. But don't go to any great effort to avoid playing the 4th string, and when playing a G⁷ chord, continue to fret the 4th string with the left hand.

At this point the beginner should consider: the rhythm of a banjo is more important than its harmony or melody. This means that in learning one should concentrate more on the right hand than the left.

Did you ever see a drummer practicing on his little rubber pad? For hours on end he will beat the same patterns, first in one tempo and then another. He cannot be merely satisfied to know 'how' a certain rhythm is to be played. He must know it so well that he can practically do it in his sleep. He must be able to hold if necessary the same tempo through a piece. No distraction, no inept fellow player should be able to knock him off his course.

The banjo player's right hand must similarly learn each pattern of strumming and picking so well that he doesn't even need to think about it. Then, if he wants to sing a song, he can concentrate on the song without worrying about the details.

Best way to get this rhythmic control is to play a lot, especially with other musicians. (Have you a friend who plays the guitar?)

Try chording along on a few familiar tunes to start with, until your left hand goes almost automatically to the right position, and the right hand is steady and relaxed.

OH SUSANNA
Words and music by Stephen Foster, 1848

```
C                                   G7
I come from Alabama with a banjo on my knee
    C                           G7    C
I'm going to Louisiana, my true love for to see
F           C           G7
O, Susanna, don't you cry for me
    C                           G7    C
I come from Alabama with a banjo on my knee
```

It rained all night, the day I left, the weather it was dry
The sun so hot I froze to death, Susanna, don't you cry.
(chorus)

THIS LAND IS YOUR LAND

(words and music by Woody Guthrie, by Ludlow Music, New York City
Used by permission)

Cho:

```
C              F                 C
This land is your land, this land is my land
          G7                   C
From California to the New York Island
                  F                    C
From the Redwood forest to the Gulf Stream water
 G7                        C
This land was made for you and me.
```

As I went walking that ribbon of highway
I saw above me that endless skyway
I saw below me that golden valley
This land was made for you and me (chorus)

I roamed and I rambled and I followed my footsteps
To the sparkling sands of her diamond deserts
While all around me a voice was sounding
This land was made for you and me (chorus)

As the sun came shining and I was strolling
And the wheat fields waving and the dust cloud rolling
As the fog was lifting a voice was chanting
This land was made for you and me (chorus)

CRAWDAD

```
C
You get a line and I'll get a pole, honey
                                    G7
You get a line and I'll get a pole, babe
 C
You get a line and I'll get a pole
F
We'll go down to the crawdad hole
C        G7       C
Honey, sugarbaby, mine.
```

Get up old man you slept too late, honey
Get up old man you slept too late, babe
Get up old man you slept too late
The crawdad man done passed your gate
Honey, sugarbaby mine.

Yonder come a man with a sack on his back, etc.
Look at them crawdads back to back, etc.

What you gonna do when the lake goes dry, etc.
Sit on the bank and watch the crawdads die, etc.

Get up old man you slept too late, etc.
I ate the last crawdad on your plate, etc.

TAVERN IN THE TOWN

```
C
There is a tavern in the town
                               G7
Where my love goes and sits him down
    C                    F
And drinks his wine as merry as can be
    G7                   C
And never, never thinks of me
```

OH MARY

Cho:
```
C                    G7
```
Oh Mary, don't you weep, don't you mourn
```
                     C
```
Oh Mary, don't you weep, don't you mourn
```
F                    C
```
Pharoah's army got drownded
```
         G7          C
```
Oh, Mary, don't you weep

If I could I surely would
Stand on the rock that Moses stood
Pharoah's army got drownded
Oh Mary, don't you weep.

Mary wore three links of chain
Every link was Jesus' name.
Pharoah's army, etc.

One of these nights about twelve o'clock
This old world's gonna reel and rock,
Pharoah's army, etc.

God told Moses what to do
To lead the Hebrew children through
Pharoah's army, etc.

Moses stood on the Red Sea shore
Smotin' the water with a two-by-four
Pharoah's army, etc.

God gave Noah the rainbow sign
No more water, but fire next time
Pharoah's army, etc.

Mary wore three links of chain
Every link was freedom's name,
Pharoah's army, etc.

The very moment I thought I was lost
The dungeon shook and the chains
 fell off.
Pharoah's army, etc.

HUSH LITTLE BABY

(as collected by Alan Lomax from
Annie Brewer, Montgomery, Ala. 1937)
```
C                    G7
```
Hush, little baby, don't say a word
```
G7                      C
```
Papa's going to buy you a mockingbird

If that mockingbird don't sing
Papa's going to buy you a diamond ring

And if that diamond ring is brass
Papa's going to buy you a looking glass

And if that looking glass gets broke
Papa's going to buy you a cart and bull

And if that cart and bull turn over
Papa's going to buy you a dog named Rover

And if that dog named Rover don't bark
Papa's going to buy you a horse and cart

And if that horse and cart fall down
You'll still be the sweetest little baby in town

SKIP TO MY LOU

```
C
```
Lou, Lou, skip to my Lou
```
G7
```
Lou, Lou, skip to my Lou
```
C
```
Lou, Lou, skip to my Lou
```
G7                 C
```
Skip to my Lou, my darling

Lost my partner what'll I do ?(3 times)
Skip to my Lou, my darling

I'll get another one prettier'n you (3)
Skip to my Lou, my darling

Flies in the sugarbowl, shoo, shoo, shoo (3)

Little red wagon, painted blue (3)

Going to Texas two by two (3)

SAINTS GO MARCHING IN

```
C
```
Oh when the saints go marching in
```
                              G7
```
Oh when the saints go marching in
```
       C              F
```
Oh Lord I want to be in that number
```
C                    G7 C
```
When the saints go marching in.

Oh when the sun refuse to shine
Oh when the sun refuse to shine
Oh Lord I want to be in that number
When the sun refuse to shine.

Oh when the moon drips red with blood, etc.

Oh when the trumpet sounds a call, etc.

Oh when the new world is revealed, etc.

Oh when the saints go marching in, etc.

PAW-PAW PATCH

```
C
```
Where oh where is little Nellie
```
G7
```
Where oh where is little Nellie
```
C
```
Where oh where is little Nellie
```
G7                 C
```
Way down yonder in the paw-paw patch.

Come on boys, let's go find her (3)
Way down yonder in the paw-paw patch.

Picking up paw-paws, put 'em in your
                            pocket (3)
Way down yonder in the paw-paw patch.

Where oh where is little Jimmy, etc.

CARELESS LOVE

```
C             G7       C
```
Love, oh love, oh careless love
```
                         G7
```
Love, oh love, oh careless love
```
                  F
```
Love, oh love, oh careless love
```
C        G7           C
```
Just see what love has done to me.

I love my mom and papa too (3 times)
I leave them both to go with you.

What oh what will mama say? (3)
When she learns I've gone astray.

It's once I wore my apron low (3)
I could scarcely keep you from my door.

But now my apron strings don't pin (3)
You pass my door and won't come in.

Love, love oh careless love (3 times)
Just see what love has done to me.

8) **Before we go on to the second lesson, a couple postscripts:**

If you are left-handed, I think nevertheless you'd find it best not to reverse the tuning or playing position; it's almost impossible, considering the peculiar place of the fifth string peg. One person I know had a special left-handed banjo made for him.

Also, you will notice that in each lesson I put down some song in music notation. If you can't read it, you should get the LP record, "Five String Banjo Instructor" which is issued as a companion piece to this manual. Without this, or a good teacher, your best bet is then to start learning to read either notation or tablature.

Music notation is basically so simple, I'd advise anyone who doesn't know to make a trip to the music store and get some beginner's manual; I have given a few rudiments in Appendix 4; knowing how to read music will make learning from this manual much easier.

A family ensemble. At far left is a dulcimer (Margot Mayo playing). Other instruments which might be used in such a group would be mandolin, French Harp (harmonica), washtub bass, pennywhistle, jaw's harp, bones, or even knitting needles tapped on the fiddle strings (while the fiddler is fiddling).

The snake in the picture is silent

SOME OLDTIMERS...

Above, right, is Samantha Bumgarner, the first person I ever heard play the 5-string banjo. It was at the Asheville Folk Festival, in 1935.

Above, left, is Rufus Crisp, of Allen, Kentucky, who taught me frailing.

CHECK LIST FOR BEGINNERS

Here are some of the most likely things to go wrong if you are just starting.

Having trouble in getting in tune? Pluck the string constantly while you gradually turn the peg. Stop turning when your ear tells you you have reached the right pitch. Use a pitch pipe or piano to help you.

It won't stay in tune long? Check for faulty pegs. Or maybe your bridge is sliding around. Glue it down with a drop of Elmer's glue along the side. Or maybe your drum is too loose.

Are your fingernails short on the left hand and long on the right? Check with Appendix 5.

Your banjo has poor tone? I'll bet either you have old strings on it, or, more likely the drum is loose, as is often the case with old instruments. Tighten it up right away!

Maybe other things are going wrong; check with Appendix 1 again.

III

THE FIFTH STRING

The thing which gives this style of banjo playing its distinctive flavor is the unusual function of the 5th string. It's the 'ring' of "hear those banjoes ringing". Like a triangle in an orchestra, it keeps on dinging away through a whole song, never changing in pitch.

The right thumb is practically always the finger that plucks the 5th string - that's why some call it the "thumb string".

In this basic strum we are learning now, the rhythm is still essentially the same as in the previous lesson. But instead of simply "one, two; one, two;" it is now "one, two-and; one, two-and, " ....the "and" is where you pluck the 5th string.

Some find it easier to count "one-two-three-four" very fast, and then keep silent on the "two". The resulting "one---three-four" is the galloping banjo sound.

> Say "bumm-titty, bumm-titty, "
> over and over to yourself; that
> is the rhythm you're aiming at.

Ground covered by this chapter (and other chapters in the book) can be heard on the LP record "The 5-String Banjo Instructor". Folkways Records, 121 W. 47 St. NYC)

If you know where you can get the use of a 16mm sound motion picture projector, you can see and hear the examples played slow as well as fast, in the 40 minute movie "The 5-String Banjo" (for sale or rent through Folkways also). See back inside cover.

Now, the first line of the song on page 7 might be played like this. (T stands for "thumb".)

THE UNION WAY

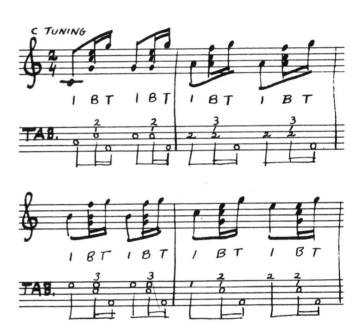

As you'll notice, the 5th string seems to come in on an off-beat. Kind of kicks off at the rear end of each beat. It never changes pitch, though strictly speaking it's not in harmony with some chords (try playing it with an F chord). Nevertheless for some curious reason, probably because it is so high up, it does not jar the ear. It's what composers call a "pedal point". Only if you play many "pop" songs, which use more than the three basic chords used by most American folksongs, will you occasionally find the wrong discords.

If you learn nothing but this one thing well, that's plenty for today's lesson. Play it over and over till it goes smoothly. Sing through the songs given in the previous chapter, and any others you know. Only now use the 5th string throughout.

Learn to play slowly as well as fast. It is the mark of an inexpert player that he is unable to slow down. Try for an even, clear rhythm, steady and relaxed.

SKIP TO MY LOU

Usually when you are singing the verses of a song, you will keep the banjo down to a simple rhythmic and harmonic accompaniment. Sometimes, though, it is quite effective to have it play the melody in unison with the voice:

Other times you may want to work out a counter melody to what the voice is singing:

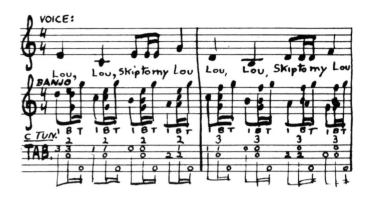

THE BLUE TAILED FLY

(Complete words and music in Kolb, "A Treasury Of Folk Songs". Bantam Books.)

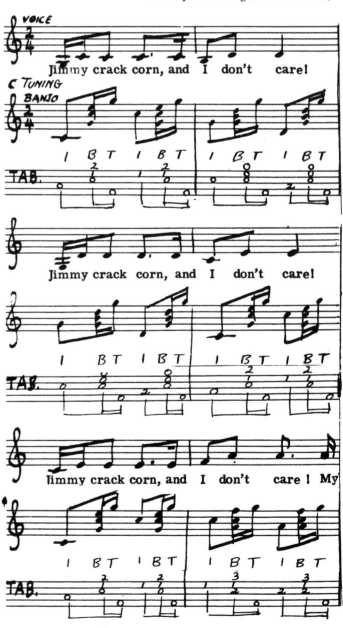

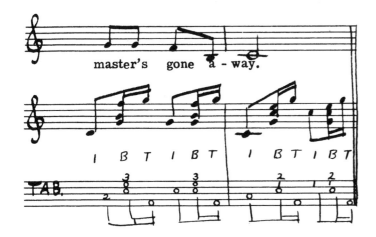

master's gone a - way.

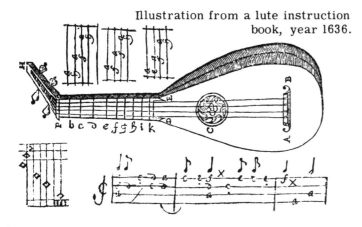

Illustration from a lute instruction book, year 1636.

HARMONY LESSON: "WHAT IS A CHORD?"

If you don't already know, I hope you are curious to find out exactly what those "chords" (pronounced KORDS) I have been talking about. . . . C, F, G, etc.

This is the first of several lessons which should give you a little of the music theory behind what you are learning. So here goes.

A song, besides having words, has melody, rhythm, and (when you have an accompaniment such as this banjo gives), harmony, which seems to reinforce, support, or otherwise back up the melody.

The harmony in our case is a series of several notes played together, which we call a chord.

Of course, just any three notes won't do. But try doing this: hum a scale to yourself. "do, re, mi, fa, sol, la, ti, do, . . or . . "one, two, three, four, five, six, seven, eight".

| 1 | 2 | 3 | 4 | 5 | 6 | 7 | 8 |
| do | re | mi | fa | sol | la | ti | do |

Now, run through the scale again, but sing out only on the 1st, 3rd, and 5th notes: if any instrument plays these three notes simultaneously, you hear a chord.

In fact, take the 1st, 3rd, and 5th of any major scale, and you have a major chord. (a minor chord differs only in that the 3rd is 1/2 tone lower).

If "1" is a C note, it's called a "C" chord (C,E,G,).

If the 1st note is G, it's a G chord.

Of course you can, and often do play the chord up-side down: 3-5-1, or 5-1-3, or spread over several octaves: 1-5-3, or 5-3-1, or 3-1-5, or with some notes repeated: 1-5-1-3, 5-1-3-1, or 1-5-3-5, etc.

But in all these variations it is still a G chord, if "1" is a G note.

Try fingering a C chord on your banjo now. Play the 4th string alone; it's "C" isn't it? That happens to be the "1" of this chord. Now play the 3rd string alone, that "G", it is the "5" of the chord. (Count up to it and see). Then try the 2nd string; originally a B, you've fretted it up a 1/2 tone to C, so here's another "1". The 1st string, originally D, is now fretted up to E, which is the "3" of the chord.

Your 5th string, being a high G, is another "5". You see how all the notes together make a C chord? 1-5-1-3-5.

Exercise: Play the F and G chords and tell me which string fulfills which part of the chord. Answers at bottom of page (don't look till you've tried).

It will be of great help to you to train your ear to know which notes are which, in any chord. If you have a piano around, try making chords, starting on any note you hit at random. First play a scale up from your chosen note (let your ear tell you when and when not to play black notes). Then play only "1" "3" and "5". Try juggling the chords around, 'inverting' them. Incidentally, whatever note is "1" is known also as the 'root' of a chord.

Summary: These chords, backing up your melody make all this mellifluous harmony you hear about. They can be added to, twisted, staggered, and juggled about, of course, to make it more interesting.

ANSWERS: For an F chord,
the 4th string is "5" or C
the 3rd string is "3" or A
the 2nd string is "5" or C
the 1st string is "1" or F
and the 5th string is "9" or "2"
(G)- not in the chord, strictly speaking, but this aberration doesn't seem to matter.

For a G chord,
the 4th string is "5" or D
the 3rd string is "1" or G
the 2nd string is "3" or B
the 1st string is "5" or D
the 5th string is "1" or G

IV

HAMMERING ON

In playing the banjo you can get some notes with your left hand. One method is to fret a string so hard you can hear it. This I call "hammering on".

For example, pluck the open 3rd string with your right forefinger, then immediately hammer down with the middle finger of your left hand on the 3rd string, just "south" of the second fret. If two other fingers were fretting a C chord, your middle finger would then be where the hollow dot is in this diagram.

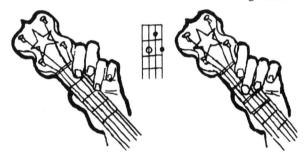

Tnen, as usual brush down on all your strings, and thumb the 5th string. Instead of sounding like "bump-ditty, bump-ditty" as in Lesson III, it should be more like "bumpa-ditty, bumpa-ditty", with the "pa" representing where you hammer down. On music paper it would look like this:

Try this hammering on in the C chord at least till it goes smoothly and easily. Say the word "Chattanooga" over and over to yourself. That's the rhythm you're aiming at.

You can do this in many places and with many different chords. When you can hammer on with force, you don't even need to pluck up on the same string beforehand. You have the general principle now. Experiment as you will.

JOHN HENRY

(For complete verses see 'American Favorite Ballads' Oak Pub. 121 W. 47, NYC

When singing the verses, don't try and play the melody at the same time. Just chord along in back of the voice, somewhat as shown below. From time to time, between the verses, the banjo can take over and play the melody by itself.

HARMONY LESSON: "WHY IS A CHORD?"

Much of music theory, since it's evolved through centuries of tradition, is completely illogical - like the clothes we wear and the food we eat, all based less upon science than upon custom. But some aspects of harmony are precise, and mathematically logical.

To illustrate: only custom dictates when or where we play a chord, but there is a very mathematical reason why the 1-3-5 of a major chord sounds pretty, and three miscellaneous other notes may not. Here's why:

First, you know that the tone you hear is the vibration of the banjo string, transmitted by the bridge to the drum, tnus to the air, and thus to our eardrums. (An A note, for example, is 440 vibrations per second).
However, rarely is a tone's vibration purely and simply that of its basic pitch; there will be minor vibrations which we call overtones. In other words, a soundwave is liable not to look so much like this:

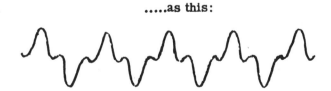

.....as this:

In the case of a vibrating string you can test this principle, and see for yourself that a string not only vibrates in one piece:

But it could be vibrating in two pieces, or three, or more, all at the same time.

Here's how: take a knife handle and rest it crosswise on the string, as a Hawaiian guitar player would. Rest it in the exact center (12th fret) - you'll now get a note just one octave higher. Rest it 1/3 the way from a bridge (use a yardstick to measure). Now you'll get a note one 5th higher. Rest it 1/4 way from the bridge, and your note will be two full octaves higher than the open string was. And try it one fifth the way from the bridge; it will be still a <u>third</u> higher!

These are the principle overtones you hear without realizing it when you pluck a string. Put them all together, and what have you? 1-1-5-1-3.......... a major chord! Of course, there are more overtones, higher up (listen to any deep bell, and you'll hear hundreds of them).

Do you see now why the 1-3-5 notes of any scale seem to make a nice sound together? It is because the 3 and the 5 reinforce the overtones of the 1, the basic note.

Incidentally, further illustration of this business of overtones can be seen in the case of the bugle. In blowing harder and pursing his lips tighter, the bugler simply gets the long column of air inside the brass tube to vibrate not in three pieces, but in four, then five, then six pieces. He gets a higher note each time, of course, notes which when put together from a major chord.

WHEN NOT TO PLAY THE BANJO

Obviously, when someone is trying to get the baby to go asleep. Nor when your neighbor, who has to be up at 6 AM to go to work, is trying to catch some much needed shut-eye.

There are other times as well, in which a sensitive musical ear can tell you to lay aside the instrument. Some types of music, after all, were simply not made for it. This goes especially for certain types of slow songs, whose effect will be spoiled by the sharp punctuation of the banjo strings.

Furthermore, in accompanying yourself in a song, you will often find it desirable to stop playing for a whole phrase, and let the voice stand alone. Then when the banjo rejoins you, it will be ever more welcome.

V

"PULLING OFF"

The left hand can also make notes by actually plucking a string (usually works most easily on the 1st, 2nd, and 3rd strings). Try it. I call it "pulling off".* You put this note in the same place you would put a note gained by hammering down. Thus, try pulling off on the 1st string. First, fret the 1st string two frets up, thus:

Then pull away with the ring finger of your left hand, thus sounding the first string.

Follow through with brushing down and thumbing the fifth string. You would get something which on music paper would look like this:

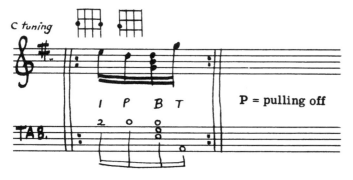

Getting a little tricky now, try this (note always which string is being plucked):

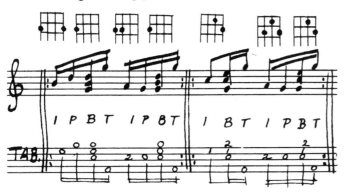

* Violinists call this "Left Hand Pizzicato".

Here is a concrete piece to try out everything you have learned so far.

The words and melody of chorus are as follows:

HARD, AIN'T IT HARD

It's hard, and it's hard, ain't it hard? To love one that never did love you! It's hard and it's hard and it's hard, Great God, to love one that never will be true.

Meanwhile, the banjo might play it this way:

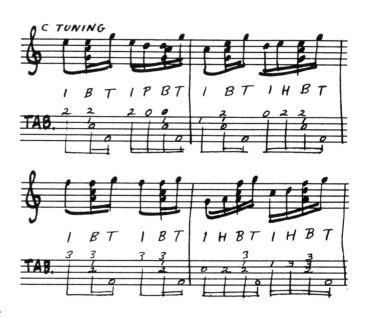

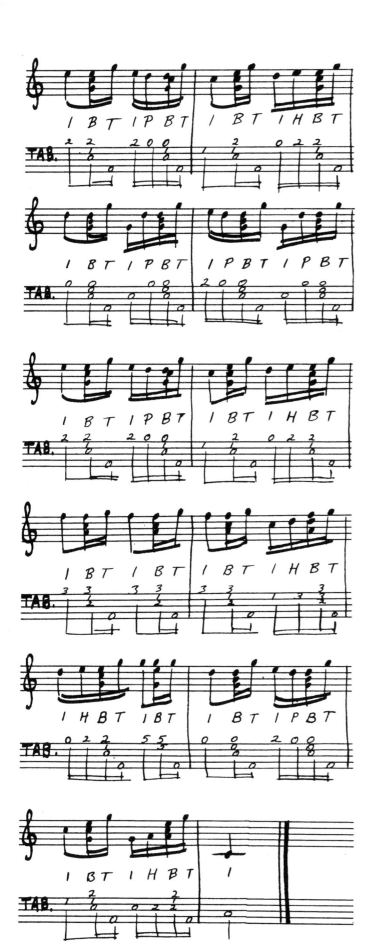

For complete words and music to this song
see "The Weaver's Songbook" (Harpers Pub.)

Harmony lesson: 6th's, 7th's, etc.

These extra notes you are adding are not always in the "1-3-5" of our original major chord. In fact, if you'll analyze it, you'll see that when you hammer down in C, you are adding the 6th note of a C scale. That extra note is an A. Count up from C and check it:

$$C-D-E-F-G-A$$
$$1-2-3-4-5-6$$

When an A is added to a C chord, then we call it a C^6 chord. There are also C^7, C^9 and even C^{13}. Look up Appendix 2 and check and few of them.

You can also lower the "3" of any major chord a 1/2 tone, and it becomes a minor chord. (Compare C and Cm, F and Fm, etc).

For additional changes, see Appendix 3. Right now, I would urge you learn G^7 and D^7, and try the following exercise: Joe Hill.

JOE HILL

By Earl Robinson and
Alfred Hayes. Complete
words and music in
"Lift Every Voice"

C   F
I dreamed I saw Joe Hill last night, alive as you and
C   C   F   C
me..... Says I, but Joe, you're ten years dead; "I
D⁷   G⁷   G⁷   C
never died," says he..... "I never died," says he...

Copyright 1938 by Bob Miller, Inc.
Used by permission

Use all the tricks you have so far learned; hum the melody and finger the right chords with your left hand.

> Incidentally, in plucking up on your single string, making the main note of your strum, try moving around a bit, using either the string which seems to sound best for a bass note, or one which becomes part of the melody. Sometimes you can play almost a complete tune with only the notes plucked up by your right index finger.

The reader may wonder at the author's annoying habit of not giving complete songs as examples. There are several reasons for this. One is the author's natural laziness. Another is lack of space in this book, which is already twice as big as it was supposed to be. More than this though: I hope the reader will be goaded into working out his own arrangements. I mention books where the rest of the words and music may be found. It's worth a trip to the public library to look them up.

VI

DOUBLE THUMBING

While the basic strum which you have presumably mastered by now is fine for simple accompaniments, and "chording" along, you may at times want to play a little more melody and fewer chords. In the middle of a song it is quite easy to break into the following, which I call "double thumbing".

(For practice sake finger a C chord with your left hand)

1 - pluck up on the first string, with right index finger
2 - with your right <u>thumb</u> pluck down on the second string
3 - pluck the first string again as before
4 - thumb the fifth string

Play these four notes over and over till they go smoothly. After a while your speed will increase so you can go from straight strumming into double thumbing without a drop in rhythm.

On music paper the above would look like this:

SKIP TO MY LOU

Now, here is the song written out for a lot of double thumbing, with an occasional strumming of chords to keep the rhythm going. Watch where you start playing high-up the neck in the end of the second measure.

It is an example of why good banjo playing has a nice, sparkling, lively quality. The melody is there, all right, but it is surrounded by a myriad of other notes. A kaleidoscopic effect is created, a brilliantly patterned carpet against which the melody carried by a voice is shown off well.

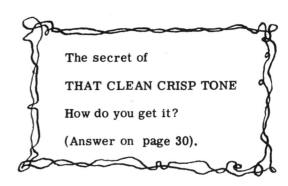

The secret of

THAT CLEAN CRISP TONE

How do you get it?

(Answer on page 30).

RETUNING TO PLAY IN 'G'

So far I have taught you only songs that are in the key of C (and using only the chords C, F, and G).

If you want to play in the key of G, you'll find it **convenient to actually retune the** instrument slightly, and use the "G tuning".

Simply tighten your 4th string one whole tone up from C to D. Brushing your hand across the open strings should give you now simply a straight G major chord.

The other chords you are liable to use when playing in the G tuning are as follows (see **Appendix 3** for more of them).

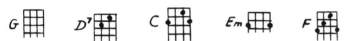

This business of retuning to play in a different key is common with folk musicians in many parts of the world. Don't think of it as "cheating"; without retuning, some pieces would be impossible to play. Even Segovia retunes a bass string occasionally.

Try playing some of the below tunes in the G tuning.

This first song is all "double thumbing".

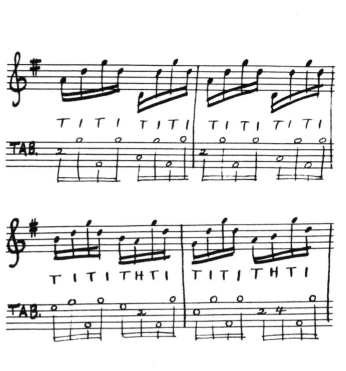

(Do you recognize the tune? It's the same one you played a few pages back in the key of C, "Hard, Ain't It Hard".)

"I used to be a pretty good singer till tunes come in fashion." (Source unknown).

Now try another song in the G tuning, but back in our first style of strumming. You'll recognize it right away: "Old Time Religion".

Some songs seem just right in the key of G. Try "Down By The Riverside", or "Oh, Mary".

G   D7
Oh, Mary, don't you weep, don't you mourn
                  G
Oh, Mary, don't you weep, don't you mourn
C   G
Pharoah's army got drownded
           D7   G
Oh, Mary, don't you weep.

Try transposing some of the other songs on page 8 and 9 to G tuning. Here's another.

WORRIED MAN BLUES

Chorus:
  G
It takes a worried man to sing a worried song
  C   G
It takes a worried man to sing a worried song

It takes a worried man to sing a worried song
                     D7   G
I'm worried now, but I won't be worried long.

I went across the river and I lay down to sleep (3 times)
When I woke up, I had shackles round my feet (chorus)

Twenty-nine links of chain around my leg (3 times)
And on each link, an initial of my name (chorus)

I asked that judge, tell me what's gonna be my fine (3)
Twenty-one years on the Rocky Mountain Line (chorus)

The train arrived twenty-one coaches long (3)
The girl I love, she's on that track and gone (chorus)

I looked down that track, just far as I could see (3)
Little bitty hand was waving after me (chorus)

If anyone should ask you who composed this song (3)
Tell 'em it was me and I sing it all day long (chorus)

BOWLING GREEN
Adapted and arranged by Joy May Creasy (Cousin Emmy)
by Joy May Creasy and Alfred Creasy

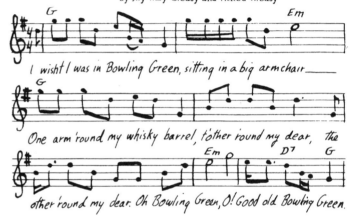

If you see that man of mine,
Tell him once for me,
If he loves another gal,
Yes, I'll set him free,
Yes, I'll set him free.

Chorus: Bowling Green --,
              O! Good old Bowling Green.

Wisht I was a bumble bee,
Sailing through the air,
Take my feller by my side,
Touch him if you dare,
Touch him if you dare.

(Chorus)

I'm going through this wide old world,
I'm going through alone,
I'm going through this wide old world,
I ain't got no home,
I ain't got no home.

(Chorus)

If you can locate an old record of Cousin Emmy singing this song, you'll hear a wonderful rendition of it. It was a 78 RPM album, Decca # A-574, called "Kentucky Mountain Ballads", now out of print.

The G tuning is especially good for square dance tunes, but for these you will want to take a look at chapters VII and VIII.

Meanwhile, as long as we are learning double thumbing, let me introduce you to still another method of tuning the banjo. It is not as commonly used by most banjo pickers, but it is unbeatable for certain songs. It is known as:

THE D TUNING

I'll assume you're already in G tuning, with the first and 4th strings both on D. Now:

Tune the 3rd string down a half tone to F#
Tune the 2nd string a whole tone down to A
Tune the 5th string down a half tone to F#
Result: DF#AD
F#

Now you can try the song "Darling Corey". For this way of playing it I am indebted to one B. F. Shelton who recorded it way back in the 20's for Victor. It was one of the first banjo tunes I ever learned, and still one of my favorites.

Here is the melody to be sung by the voice...the rhythm is very steady, but the metre is very irregular. No two verses should be exactly alike.

DARLING COREY

Wake up, wake up! Darling Corey!
What makes you sleep so sound? The
Revenue officers are comin'
Gonna tear your still house down!

Well, the first time I seen Darling Corey
She was sitting by the banks of the sea
She had a forty five strapped around her waist
And a banjo on her knee.

Well, the last time I seen Darling Corey,
She had a dram glass in her hand
She was drinking down her troubles
With a no good gambling man.

Wake up, wake up, Darling Corey
Go do the best you can
I've got me another woman
You can hunt you another man.

Oh, yes, Oh yes, my darling
I'll do the best I can
But I'll never give my troubles
To another gambling man.

Dig a hole, dig a hole in the meadow
Dig a hole in the cold cold ground
Dig a hole, dig a hole in the meadow
Gonna lay Darling Corey down.

During the singing of each verse Shelton held to a driving rhythm of just two notes repeated over and over:

In between the verses from time to time he played
(Continued on next page)

For recordings of the banjo with a lot of double thumbing, listen to some of the following:
"Pickin' and Blowin'" (Riverside 12-650)
"Mountain Music of Kentucky" (Folkways 2317)
See also Library of Congress recordings, mentioned on page 72.

the melody on the banjo, as follows:

DARLING COREY

On the other side of the record where I learned this song, Shelton sings a fine gory ballad "Pretty Polly" - also with a double thumbing accompaniment. The words and music to "Darling Cory" as given here, can be found in a folio called "The Goofing Off Suite" published by Hargail Music Press, 157 W. 57 St. NYC. The folio includes another banjo piece in D tuning, which I learned from Pete Steele, The Coal Creek March.

The advantage of retuning a banjo is to get certain effects unobtainable otherwise. "You want to get as many open strings as you can", said Buell Kazee once to a friend of mine. The disadvantage, which you will find out if you play for audiences of any size, is that your listeners will become restive while they wait for you to retune. However, folk musicians do it all the time. Some banjo players invent new tunings as they need them, and a particularly successful one is imitated. Rufus Crisp, of Allen, Kentucky, knew some eighteen.

For convenient playing in any key under the sun, though, there is nothing quite so handy as a device known as a capo:

HARMONY LESSON: THE CAPO

If you have not already bought a banjo capo, do so now - they cost only a few cents. With its help you can very simply play a song in <u>any</u> key you want.

For supposing you are a tenor or a soprano, and in your songbook you find some song written, say, in the key of C - and it seems too low for your voice. Perhaps you'd rather sing it in D. All right, you have a capo already around the neck of your banjo, as shown at right. Just move it up the neck two frets, letting it rest just "south" of the frets, where you would normally put your fingers.

Now retune your 5th string a similar amount higher (from G to A).

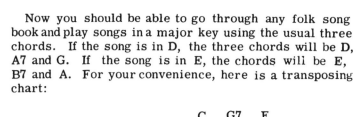

Now you can go ahead and play the song in C, except that you will really be in a key more suited to your voice, the key of D. When your left hand makes a G^7 chord, you'll really be in A^7, and so on.

If the key of C is too high for your voice, on the other hand, and you'd rather sing the song down in A, retune to a "G tuning", and move the capo up two frets and play G, C, and D^7 chords - but really you'll be playing A, D, and E^7 chords.

It's like Irving Berlin's famous piano, which he had specially built; he cranks the keyboard up and down, so he can pitch a tune just right for his voice - although he himself can only play in one key.

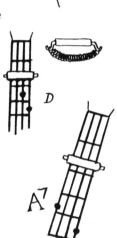

I myself practically never play except in G or C - and with the use of a capo, can make it come out E♭, or G♯, or anything else needed. Again, don't think of it as 'cheating'.

Now you should be able to go through any folk song book and play songs in a major key using the usual three chords. If the song is in D, the three chords will be D, A7 and G. If the song is in E, the chords will be E, B7 and A. For your convenience, here is a transposing chart:

C	G7	F
C#	G#7	F#
D♭	A♭7	G♭
D	A7	G
E♭	B♭7	A♭
E	B7	A
F	C7	B♭
G♭	D♭7	C♭ (B)
G	D7	C
A♭	E♭7	D♭
A	E7	D
B♭	F7	E♭
B	F#7	E

For all these fancy chords, you can just read them as "C, G7 and F", or "G, D7, and C" depending on how you use your capo.

One note: the 5th string will break if you try to tighten it up more than one tone higher than its intended pitch. Therefore, you must do one of two things: put a small screw in the fingerboard under which you can slip the string. artificially fretting it; or else devise some 5th string capo. In any case, see Appendix 2 for directions.

Also, if the cork padding on your capo wears out (it will), cut off a short piece of bathroom shower hose and slip it over the bar. It works even better. Some use a similar tube to keep the spring from scratching varnish off the neck.

To prove to yourself just how important it is to sing in the right key, take any song you know and try singing it in as many keys as your capo and two banjo tunings can give you. You'll rapidly see that some are completely impossible. Either you growl and whisper on the low notes, or squeak on the high ones. Of the few practical keys, you'll find the lower ones are best if you want to sing softly, calmly. But if you want to sing more spiritedly, or loudly, you'll pitch the song higher. People sing higher when out-of-doors, for example.

When learning a song, one of your first jobs is therefore to find where to pitch it so that it suits your voice and if you want others to sing with you, where it suits their voices.

Roscoe Holcomb   photo by John Cohen

Try putting your capo up two frets and playing the following as though it were in G. Actually you'll be playing A, E7, and D, although you simply finger the chords for G, D7 and C.

THE SINKING OF THE REUBEN JAMES
Written by Woodie Guthrie in 1941

```
     A                        E7         A
Have you heard of a ship called the good Reuben James?
                              E7         A
Manned by hard fighting men both of honor and fame
                              D          A
She flew the stars and stripes of the land of the free
                              E7         A
But tonight she's in her grave at the bottom of the sea.
```

Chorus:

```
                                   D
Tell me, what were their names, tell me what were
                                     their names?
   E7                      A
Did you have a friend on the good Reuben James?
                                   D
Tell me, what were their names, tell me what were
                                     their names?
   E7                      A
Did you have a friend on the good Reuben James?
```

It was there in the dark of that uncertain night
That we watched for the U-boats and waited for the fight
Then a whine and a rock and a great explosion roared
And they laid the Reuben James on that cold ocean floor.

(chorus)

One hundred men were drowned in that dark watery grave
When that good ship went down only forty four were saved
Twas the last day of October that we saved the forty four
From the cold icy waters off the cold Iceland shore.

(chorus)

Now tonight there are lights in our country so bright
In the farms and in the cities they are telling of that fight
And now our mighty battleships will steam the bound-
ing main
And remember the name of that good Reuben James.

Fred Hellerman of the Weavers has added a nice last verse:

Well, many years have passed since those brave men
have gone
And those cold icy waters are still and they're calm
Many years have passed but still I wonder why
The worst of men must fight and the best of men must
die.

THE OLD BARN FLOOR. Large folio Currier and Ives, 1868.

You sharpen up your sense of pitch every time you have to tune a banjo. Here's a little diversion to sharpen your sense of rhythm. Get someone who knows how to read music to help you. Remember that two quick "eighth notes" (♫) take up the same amount of time as one ordinary "quarter note". And that two extra quick "sixteenth notes" (♬) equal one eighth note (♪).

A LITTLE RHYTHM PRACTICE:

1) Try clapping 2/4 time, march rhythm.

Do it over and over, emphasizing the first clap in each measure.

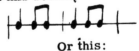

2) Now, if two 1/8 notes equal one 1/4 note, how would this sound:

Or this:

3) This would be simple:

4) But can you clap this?

5) O.K. For a final exam:

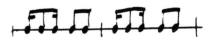

24

VII

3/4 AND 6/8 TIME

Up to now all our practice examples have been in simple 2/4 or 4/4 time, fast or slow. However, at least two other rhythms are very common in American folkmusic, and you'd best become acquainted with them.

First, 3/4, or waltz time; for this you simply repeat the second stroke in strumming, as follows:

1) a-pluck up on a single string, with index finger.
   b-hammer down or pull off with left hand.
2) a-brush down across all strings.
   b-thumb the fifth string.
3) a-brush down across all strings.
   b-again thumb the 5th string.

This can be done fast or slow, of course. Here is a typical example of 3/4 time ("Down In the Valley"), which I have written down to make use of double thumbing as well.

* This chapter is differently arranged than in the second edition. Material has been added but none has been cut out. See page 47.

Here are the first verses to some of my own favorite songs in 3/4 time.   Try working them out yourself. Complete words are given in some of the books listed on page 71.

      C   F   C
On top of Old Smokey . . all covered with snow. .
                            G7   C
I lost my true lover.. for courting too slow.. etc.

    C
As I was a-walking the streets of Laredo
    C   G7   C   G7
As I was a-walking Laredo one day,
    C   G7   C   G7
I spied a young cowboy all wrapped in white linen
    C   F   G7   C
All wrapped in white linen, as cold as the clay.   *

               C
O, brandy, leave me alone,
                              F
O, brandy, leave me alone,
                              G7
O, brandy leave me alone,
                              C
Remember, I must go home.   *

       C
There was an old farmer who went out to plow,
F   C
Tee roo, tee roo, who went out to plow,
                              G7
With sixteen oxen and a darned old cow,
                          C
Tee roo, tee roo, and a darned old cow.   *

           C
Last night I had the strangest dream,
  F   C
I never dreamed before,
  G7   C
I dreamed the world had all agreed,
    F   G7   C
To put an end to war.   *

G
I ride an old paint, I lead an old Dan,
D7   G
I'm going to Montana to throw the Hooliyan,
D7   G
They feed 'em in the coulees, they water in the draw,
D7   G
Their tails are all matted, their backs are all raw.

G   D7   G   D7   G   D7
De la Sierra Morena Cielito Lindo vienen bajando

                                                           G
Un par de ojitos negros Cielito Lindo los contrabando

         C   D7   G
Ay - ay - ay- ay; canta y no llores.

                         D7
Porque, cantando se alegran, Cielito Lindo los

            G
       corazones.

          G   D7   G
    Irene Goodnight, Irene, goodnight,

                     C
   Goodnight Irene, goodnight Irene,

      D7   G
   I'll see you in my dreams.   *

     G
As I was a-walking down Paradise Street

               D7
To my way, hey, blow the man down,

A pretty young damsel I chanced for to meet,

                    G
Give me some time to blow the man down

     Cm   B♭
    Alas, my love you do me wrong,

     C m   G7
   To cast me off discourteously,

     Cm   B♭
   When I have suffered, Oh so long,

     Cm   G7   Cm
   Delighting in your company.

    E♭   B♭
   Greensleeves was all my joy,

    Cm   G7
   Greensleeves was my delight,

    E♭   B♭
   Greensleeves was my heart of gold,

     Cm   G7   Cm
   And who but my lady Greensleeves?

(see page 65 for chords)

  G   C
We wish you a Merry Christmas

  A7   D 7
We wish you a Merry Christmas

  G   C
We wish you a Merry Christmas

  D7   G
And a Happy New Year.

      C   G7
   As I sat down one evening
                        C
   Within a small cafe
                    F
   A forty year old waitress
     G7   C
   To me these words did say..   *

           C   G7   C
O have you heard tell of Sweet Betsy from Pike?

                                       G
She crossed the wide mountains with her lover, Ike.

  C   F   C
With two yoke of oxen and one yellow dog,

                          G7   C
A tall Shanghai rooster and a big spotted hog.

                        G7   C
Hoodle dang fol, de dido, hoodle dang fol, dee-day.

          C
   So long, it's been good to know you,
   G7   C
   So long, it's been good to know you,
                         F
   So long, it's been good to know you,
     C   G7
   This dusty old dust is a-getting my home..
                            C
   And I got to be drifting along.   *

To find the rest of the verses of all these
songs, look through some of the folksong
books listed on page 71.

Sometimes the song will sound best if you accompany it almost entirely with double thumbing. Other times you may just use straight chords. Sometimes, when the 3/4 rhythm is very slow, but still needs a good deal of straightforward drive, I double up the rhythm as follows:

CLEMENTINE

Other songs which can stand this sort of treatment are "Hallelujah I'm A-Travelling" and "Die Gedanken Sind Frei".

 There are still other ways of accompanying songs in 3/4 time. See pages 44 and 47.

6/8 TIME

6/8 time is the same as that of an Irish Jig, such as "The Irish Washer Woman". "Johnny Comes Marching Home" is also in 6/8 time. You may even find it handy to use this method for certain marches, such as "John Brown's Body".

In 6/8 time there are two strong beats to each measure, but each beat is divided into three pieces, thus: one-two-three, four-five-six; one-two-three, four-five-six.

On the banjo, you'll find it difficult to play much melody in 6/8 time; the most you can hope for is to get the rhythm and the chords, and an occasional note of the melody.

Forget about using the 5th string in its former capacity; if you pluck it at all, it will be as a downbeat, not an offbeat. Here is one way a 6/8 strum might go:
The strum should be as follows:

1) a-pluck up with the index finger on a single string
   b-hammer on or pull off with the left hand
   c-brush down across all strings
2) a-pluck up with index finger on a single string
   b-hammer on or pull off with the left hand
   c-brush down across all string

Here is a sample passage (can be used for "Rambling Wreck From Georgia Tech" - although G is a bad key to sing it in. C's better).

Most Americans have a poorly developed sense of rhythm (compared to people in Asia, Africa, South America, etc.) So see if you can test yourself, leafing through a songbook, guessing what time different songs are in. How many songs do you know in 6/8 time?

While 6/8 time is the same time as an Irish Jig, a hornpipe, though written as 4/4 time, is very similar, and can be played the same way. A hornpipe is really just 6/8 very fast. Occasionally you'll find it written as 12/8 time.

Come to think of it, in England they call that last tune "Son Of A Gambolier" and have a fine parody of it which starts off thus:

THE MAN WHO WATERS THE WORKERS' BEER

Words by Paddy Ryan ©

The waltz, as played in America and Europe, is usually pretty much of an oom-pah-pah affair. In Latin America, Africa, and in India, however, some beautiful rhythmic variations are often introduced within the basic 3/4 time structure. Consider, for example, the possibilities of such 3/4 rhythms as these, if translated to the banjo.

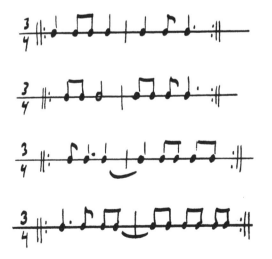

Further, when you and your guitar player friends (I assume you have some!) are playing together, you might try counter rhythms. This is as much fun as

27

singing in harmony. For example, if he is in 6/8 time, you might try your own accompaniment in 3/4. Here's a f'rinstance:

MEXICAN HAT DANCE

(Index finger plucks up throughout)

SINGLE STRING WORK: TRIPLETS

Even when playing in 2/4 or 4/4 time one sometimes wants to play a triple rhythm. Instead of dividing an eighth note into two pieces, as is usually done, it may be divided into three pieces - gives nice variety.

Here is an example: Suppose you have been chording along in the key of C. A break in the singing occurs. Let the banjo do some single string work with triplets, as shown below. Watch carefully to see which finger plucks up on which string.

Note: "Triplets" can, of course, be of several kinds besides the ones demonstrated above. For example in a 4/4 measure, one might play three quarter notes in place of the first two, thus: (Recognize it?)

Sometimes the triplets can tumble upon each other so fast that they almost give the effect of a tone cluster. Here is a favorite song of mine. (Rest of the words can be found in "Best Loved American Folksongs" A. Lomax)

LEATHERWING BAT

Hi, said the little leatherwing bat
I'll tell you the reason that
The reason that I fly by night
Is 'cause I've lost my heart's delight
  Owdeedow, adiddle um day
  Owdeedow, a diddle um day
  Owdeedow, a diddle um day
  And a hey lee lee........leelileelo!

Melody for voice:

Banjo interlude between verses:

VIII

FRAILING

Up until now we have spent all our time learning one basic method of strumming with the right hand. Let's try another method now, one which is even more commonly used. It's good for playing a fast, steady rhythm for square dances. I've heard it variously called "beating" a banjo, "frailing", "rapping", "framing" the banjo.

Essentially the difference between the two methods is this: whereas in the first method the right hand "up, down, up, down", in frailing, all notes are plucked by the back of the fingernail as the hand moves downward; thus the movements of the right hand are all "down, down, down, down".

The notes you are playing may be exactly the same on paper as before, but you'll find they sound differently. You can get a good deal more incisive punch and attack when you frail a banjo.

Here's a blow-by-blow comparison of the two systems:

"*M*" means pick down with the back of the fingernail of either the index finger or middle finger.

BASIC STRUM:	FRAILING:
1) The index finger plucks up on a single string.	1) With the back of the fingernail of the index or middle* finger pick down on a string. Move the whole forearm.
2) The left hand hammers on or pulls off on a string.	2) Same as in 1st method - left hand hammering on or pulling off.
3) The right hand brushes down across all the strings.	3) The right hand picks down across all strings (or possibly just the first two or three) and at the same time the right thumb comes to rest on the 5th string.
4) The thumb plucks the 5th string.	4) While the right hand is on the way up, the thumb pulls away from the 5th string, sounding it.

* I usually use my middle finger, because I often wear fingerpicks (see page 68.) My fingernails wear out if I don't. But my sister Peggy feels that you can never get that "nice plunky tone" with picks on. If you are not wearing finger picks, you still might like to alternate, using the index finger for the lower strings, and the middle finger for the 1st string.

It took me about three or four months to get this down smoothly, so don't be impatient. What seems hardest is to learn to place your thumb on the 5th string on the way down, and pluck it on the way up. You might try doing that one thing over and over, as an exercise, till it comes easy:

1) Brush down across all strings with back of index finger, at same time placing thumb on 5th string.

2) On the way back, pluck 5th string. ......do this over and over.

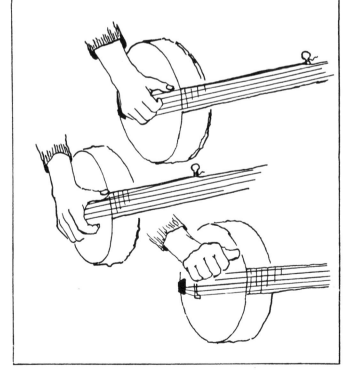

You will gradually improve your aim so your fingernail can hit the right melody string. Try to get a clean, crisp rhythm; the fingernail should brush toward the drum when it strikes a single string, and then come to rest against the adjacent string, or the drumhead itself. Don't just flip your fingers out; use whole forearm. Unless I am double thumbing while frailing, I also find it strengthens my index finger to support it with the thumb during step (1) above.

If you haven't already studied Appendix 5, do so now. You cannot frail a banjo properly unless your fingernails are the right length, or you wear fingerpicks.

Frailing works out best for 2/4 time, fast. It's less useful for other rhythms.

Double thumbing can also be done in this new system. It's much harder at first, but in the end you can do it quicker and more definitely than the other way.

FOR PRACTICE try playing some of the following measures over and over again:

There was one fine, simple lick Rufus Crisp showed me which I'll never forget. Useful any time you simply want to chord in the key of G.

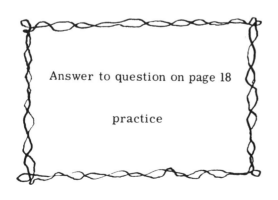

Answer to question on page 18

practice

Here is one of the world's best banjo tunes for you. Try to learn it all the way through. A piece made of, by, and for banjo pickers.

CRIPPLE CREEK

SL = slide (On these slides you see above, move the left hand firmly up the fingerboard. Fret the string for the lower note, and without releasing pressure, move it up two frets.)

Here is another famous hoedown melody especially suited for frailing. In the version I have set down here I have included a number of unisons, where two strings play the same note. This is a nice effect, and you might experiment with it further.

OLD JOE CLARK

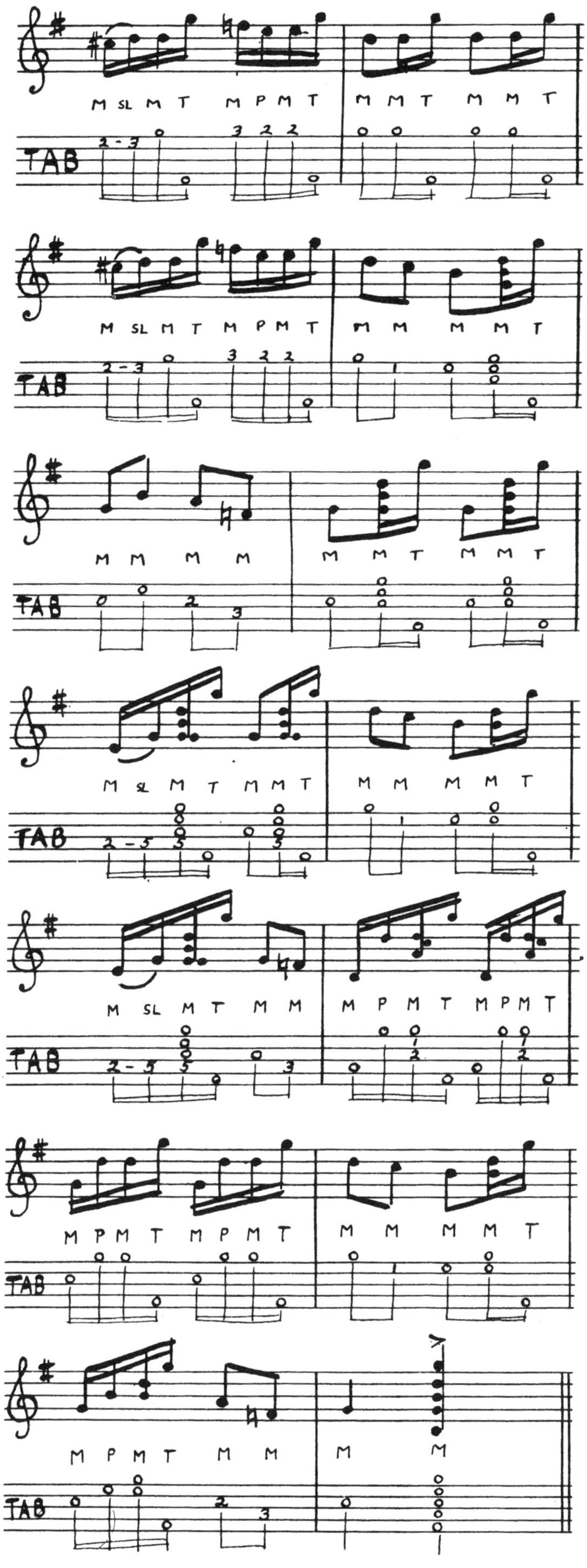

OLD JOE CLARK

The tune has hundreds of verses, a few of which we give below. Joe Clark was an actual person, a veteran of the war of 1812, who was given, in lieu of back pay, some land in the western slopes of the Blue Ridge Mountains. He raised two dozen children and they carried on the tradition.

Old Joe Clark, the preacher's son,
Preached all over the plain,
The only text he ever knew
Was "high, low jack and the game."

Old Joe Clark had a mule,
His name was Morgan Brown,
And every tooth in that mule's head
Was sixteen inches around.

Old Joe Clark had a yellow cat,
She would neither sing or pray,
She stuck her head in the buttermilk jar
And washed her sins away.

Old Joe Clark had a house,
Fifteen stories high,
And every story in that house
Was filled with chicken pie.

I went down to old Joe's house,
He invited me to supper,
I stumped my toe on the table leg
And stuck my nose in the butter.

Now I wouldn't marry a widder,
Tell you the reason why,
She'd have so many children
They'd make those biscuits fly.

Sixteen horses in my team,
The leaders they are blind,
And every time the sun goes down
There's a pretty girl on my mind.

Eighteen miles of mountain road
And fifteen miles of sand,
If I ever travel this road again,
I'll be a married man.

I wish I had a sweetheart
I'd put her on a shelf,
And every time she'd smile at me,
I'd get up there myself.

Well, I wouldn't marry that old maid,
I'll tell you the reason why,
Her neck's so long and stringy, boys,
I fear she'd never die.

And I wouldn't marry an old school teacher,
Tell you the reason why,
She blows her nose in old corn bread,
And calls it pumpkin pie.

31

Some other good hoedowns to try frailing in the key of G are: "Sally Ann", "Leather Breeches", "Sourwood Mountain", "Bile Them Cabbage Down", "Cumberland Gap", "Ground Hog", "Cindy", "Black-Eyed Susie" and "Ida Red".

There's a wild little banjo tune called "Jinny Git Around" which uses a variant of the G tuning. Lower the second string one whole tone to A. If you like the tune, you can find complete words and music in "Our Singing Country" (Lomax, MacMillan Pub.) Watch the repeat marks to see you don't repeat the wrong sections.

JINNY GIT AROUND

✲ See p. 67 for explanation of repeats ([1.]).

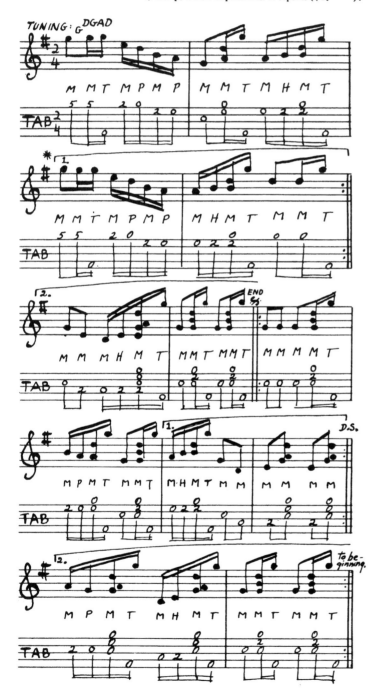

Frank Proffitt, of Reese, North Carolina, with his homemade, fretless banjo. He taught "Tom Dooley" to Frank Warner of New York City, who taught it to the rest of us. He also makes a limited number of this homemade style, for sale.

The 2nd string can also be lowered for the C tuning. Lily May Ledford of the Coon Creek Girls, a trio that used to play on the Renfrew Valley Barn Dance, used it to play a song called "Little Birdie". The 4th string goes down to C, and the 2nd string down to A. Result: G CGAD.

LITTLE BIRDIE

(The complete banjo transcription has been made by Hally Wood Stephenson and is printed in a 1961 issue of Sing Out Magazine, 121 W. 47 St. NYC. Also has all verses and melody for voice.)

In the regular C tuning, you might try "John Henry". Incidentally, the traditional way to sing a ballad such as this is to play it through once or twice on the banjo, and then sing a verse, with the banjo just playing simple chords, and rather quietly, at that, so as not to drown out the words..

JOHN HENRY

The complete verses I usually sing to this song are printed in the book "American Favorite Ballads" (Oak Publications, 121 West 47 St. NYC).

When singing the verses, you can again chord along behind them somewhat in the fashion described on page 15.

Also in C tuning is a number I first heard on a record, "The Cumberland Mt. Deer Race" by Uncle Dave Macon. Over years of singing it, I developed a little story to go with it. His original record is out of print. Let's hope some sensible pirate will reissue it one of these years. Curiously enough I once met in Los Angeles a woman who listened to the song and said, "Why, when I was a child in Czechoslovakia we used to sing that tune. But we had different words: Holka modro-oka Ne koukejse do potoka, holka modro-oka ne koukejse tam. It means, blue-eyed girl, don't look into the brook." How the tune ever got to Tennessee I couldn't

A well known musician in the commercial 'country music' field is "Grandpa Jones", who sticks strictly to the oldfashioned frailing style of banjo picking. (he calls it 'rapping' a banjo). He has published a good instruction book.

say, but obviously our songs, like our people, come from everywhere.

THE CUMBERLAND MOUNTAIN BEAR CHASE

Story and arrangement
by Peter Seeger, © 1961

CHORUS

VERSE

Chorus:
Away, away, we're bound for the mountain,
Bound for the mountain, bound for the mountain,
Away to the chase away, away.

Verse:
    Listen to the hound dog's heavy bay,
    Sounding high over the way.
    All night long till the break of dawn,
    Merrily the chase goes on.
    Over the mountain, the hills and the fountain,
    Away to the chase away, away.

(Play the chorus again on the banjo)

Verse:
    Rover, Rover, see him see him,
    Rover, Rover, catch him, catch him,
    Over the mountain, the hills and the fountain,
    Away to the chase away, away.

(Play the chorus again on the banjo, then the story begins. Keep the banjo strumming in the background.)

"Once there was a little boy, whose father used to go out hunting. He begged and he begged his father to take him along, but always the answer was 'No, you're too young, son. Stay home.' That's the way they are. But the boy kept after him until the father said 'All right, all right, I'll take you after your next birthday. Not now.' He thought the boy would forget, but he didn't. His next birthday rolled around, and he reminded his father of his promise. "All right (grudgingly), you can come. But don't expect me to slow down for you. And if you get lost up on the mountain, don't expect me to come and lead you home by the hand.' The boy replies: 'That's all right. I'll take along my horn. And if I get lost I'll blow that horn, and old Blue - the lead dog, he'll hear me and come show me the way.

"So off they went (banjo speeds up). But you know, he couldn't keep up. They got farther and farther ahead of him, till he could hardly hear them. Then he couldn't hear them at all (banjo fades to silence). He took out his horn and he blew it.

34

(Sings): "Old Blue, where are you? Old Blue where are you?"

"But all he could hear was a hoot owl" (banjo plays)

' Till way off in the distance he thought he heard something: "

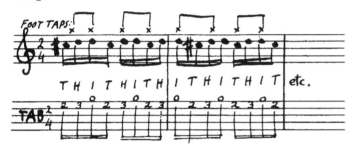

"They're coming back" he cries. "Right around the mountain again. Right to where I am!" (banjo starts strumming)

(Sing original verse and chorus again, as in beginning).

(Spoken): "Now listen to old Crickety gettin' on the trail!"

(Spoken): "I think Bugle Boy's got it now. Smart old dog!"

"Up the holler! Over the mountain!" (Banjo gets fainter)

"Now listen to those hounds bay! I believe they got him treed!" (Banjo loud again)

The imitation of hounds barking above is done by "choking" the string (letters CH). The string is stretched with the left hand so it raises in pitch while still vibrating. See page 40 for fuller description.

(Song, but not story, recorded by me in Folkways LP FA2003. Eric Darling has also recorded it for Electra.)

Below is a picture of the late "Uncle Dave Macon", in a characteristic pose. In the 1890's he performed in travelling tent shows. During the last twenty years of his life he was a regular feature on the "Grand Old Opry" radio programs. His repertoire ranged from centuries-old ballads and courting tunes, to comic ditties, work songs, topical songs about striking coalminers and sharecropping farmers, hymns and gospel songs. May he liven up the heavenly band!

HARMONY LESSON: "MOUNTAIN MINOR" TUNING

You may not have realized it, but there are many different kinds of major and minor scales. They're called "modes", and we often run across many unusual ones in folk music. One minor mode in particular is common in parts of the southern mountains, and there is a particularly charming tuning used for accompanying songs in this mode. Here it is:

First put your banjo in a G tuning: G^{DGBD}. Now raise the 2nd string from B to C (a half tone), and there you are: G^{DGCD}.

Remember, you have to change all your chords now, to compensate for the change.

The following song uses this tuning. I first heard it in a 1938 field recording made by Alan Lomax, of Walter Williams of Salyersville, Kentucky. As in the song "Darling Cory", the banjo keeps a steady, fast rhythm, though the voice part should be very irregular, with some notes held out for several extra beats. The banjo starts first, and then the voice leaps on like a rider on to a galloping horse.

EAST VIRGINIA
(Melody for voice)

I was born and raised in East Virginia,
North Carolina I did go,
And there I met the prettiest little maiden,
Her name and age I did not know.

Her hair it was of a light brown color,
Cheeks they were a rosy red,
And on her breast she wore white lilies,
Where I longed to lay my head.

I'd rather be in some dark holler,
Where the sun would never shine,
Than to see you with another,
And to know you'd never be mine.

Well, on her feet she wears little slippers,
On her hair she wears a bow.
Oh, the way I love that brown eyed darling
Nobody on earth shall never know.

I was born and raised in East Virginia,
North Carolina I did go,
And there I met that pretty little maiden,
Her name and age I do not know.

(The exact tune and words of Walter Williams were transcribed by Ruth Crawford Seeger for the Lomax book, "Our Singing Country". You can hear me performing the song as best I can on the Folkways LP "Darling Corey".)

EAST VIRGINIA
(Banjo break before and after verses)

Since many of these old ballads were sung without any accompaniment, there is no urgent need to put rich harmonies to them now; the next song is a good example. It would be hard to say for certain whether the song is in G major or E minor. As far as we are concerned, it doesn't matter, if we simply want to learn the beautiful way it has been sung by Buell Kazee, Baptist preacher of Morehead, Kentucky. This song was recorded by him on a now out-of-print Brunswick 78 rpm. Folkways Records has a more recently recorded 12" LP of him. As before, the meter of the verses is irregular, with no two verses exactly alike.

LADY GAY

There was a la—dy, and a lady gay. Of children she had three.___ She sent them away to the North countree___ for to learn their grammarree___

They had not been there very long,
Scarcely six months and a day,
Till death, cold death, came hasting along
And stole those babes away.

It was just about old Christmas time,
The nights being cold and clear,
She looked and she saw her three little babes
Come running home to her.

She set a table both long and wide
And on it she put bread and wine.
"Come eat, come drink, my three little babes;
Come eat, come drink of mine."

"We want none of your bread, mother,
Neither do we want your wine;
For yonder stands our Saviour dear,
And to him we must resign.

"Green grass grows over our heads, mother,
Cold clay is under our feet.
And every tear you shed for us,
It wets our winding sheet."

LADY GAY

(Banjo part as played by Buell Kazee)

Buell Kazee often plays the melody right along with his voice. I have transcribed half of the song here, and trust you will be able to work out the second half yourself. Tune your banjo in still another variant of the G tuning. The first four strings remain the same, but the 5th string comes down to E. Result: $_E$DGBD.

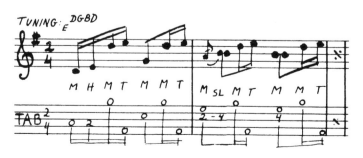

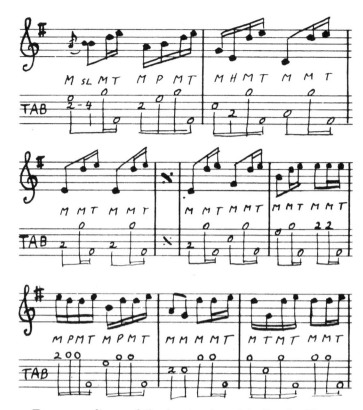

For recordings of the banjo played in the frailing style, try some of the following:
  Buell Kazee (Folkways 3810)
  Cousin Emmy (on English Brunswick 9258, 9259
        can be ordered by mail)
  Bascom Lunsford (Folkways 2040)
  Uncle Dave Macon (in Folkways Anthology FP251-3)
  See also page 72

Buell Kazee (photo from an old Brunswick record advertisement)

IX

THREE FINGER PICKING AND BLUEGRASS BANJO

If you are able to play much with other musicians, such as guitarists and fiddlers, you will want to play fewer full chords; you'll appreciate the sparkling punctuation of single strings. You may try more double thumbing (see Chapter VI) or single string work (Chapter X), but it is hard to beat the syncopated brilliance of what is known these days as 'bluegrass banjo'.

In 1945 the 5-string banjo had been abandoned by all but the most old-fashioned commercial country string bands. Then a young man named Earl Scruggs got a job with Bill Monroe and His Bluegrass Boys, playing on radio station WSM, Nashville, Tenn. Scruggs had been playing the banjo since the age of six, and when he was a teen-ager he had worked out a syncopated variation on the old 'clawhammer' fingerpicking style. Within three years he and Lester Flatt had a band of their own, playing on the Grand Old Opry, and the Gibson Company was back in the banjo business, supplying the thousands of young people wanting to imitate his style.

The style involves the thumb and two fingers of the right hand. Instead of playing chords, you work out various intricate and syncopated patterns of single strings. Try your hand at some of the following. Incidentally, it is customary to rest the little finger of the right hand (and sometimes the ring finger as well) on the drumhead, to gain steadiness.

And here is still another development of the same idea:

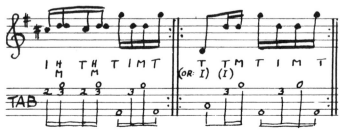

As you see, the eight 1/16th notes are continually being divided up, (as in the Rhumba, and other African-derived rhythms,) into 3-3-2. Now try this:

There are many other possible variations. One can reverse the order of the three, for example: Thumb, Middle finger, then Index finger. What it boils down to is that in playing along in the background with other musicians, you let them take the basic, or 'straight' beat while you outline the chords or countermelodies in irregular fashion. (Other instruments playing with you are almost essential, if this 3-finger style is to sound at its best).

If you play a melody, you must adapt it in a syncopated way, quite different from the way you had to adapt it in frailing. Take the melody of "Cindy". The first line might be sung as follows:

Frailing you might play that line thus:

With three fingers it might be done this way:

Because you have three fingers working for you instead of two, as in double thumbing, you can get 50% greater speed. Stands to reason. And probably such lightning-fast, hard-as-nails banjo has never been heard before. The dangers, ofcourse, are that if you don't watch it, it can start sounding mechanical and meaningless - which happens to any art form when you concentrate solely on technique and forget the content. Some people can't stand bluegrass banjo; some live only for it. My suggestion is that if you are interested, drop around to a record store and listen to some of the records listed on page 45. Then, if you want, try working your way through a couple of the pieces written on the next five pages.

Keep in mind that a bluegrass band customarily includes both guitar and bass fiddle, to give a rock steady rhythm for the banjo to dance around on top of. Witnout some rhythmic base the banjo might sound too scattered and wild. In addition, there is usually a fiddle and mandolin to share the solos with the banjo. An un-electrified steel Dobro guitar plays in "The Foggy Mountain Boys" with Scruggs.

FOGGY MOUNTAIN BREAKDOWN

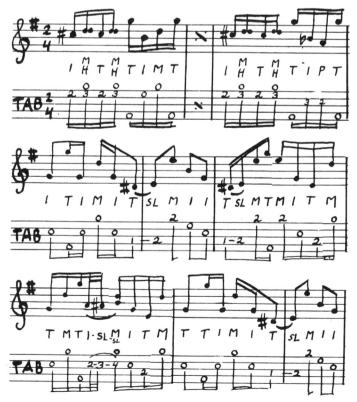

More on page 40 ➜

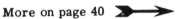

Earl Scruggs   Photo by David Gahr

The banjo pieces in this chapter were all painstakingly transcribed slowing the record down to a growl. We think we got most of the notes down correctly, but we couldn't swear that the tablature or fingering is right, because sometimes there are several possible ways of getting the same note. Some bluegrass banjo pickers prefer not to bring their thumb over to the second and third strings as often as Scruggs does. Keep in mind too, that Scruggs probably never plays the piece note by note the same way twice. He is always coming up with new ideas. Your aim should also be to get so familiar with the idiom that you can improvise within it.

FOGGY MOUNTAIN BREAKDOWN
(Variations up the neck)

After the banjo has played through the main theme a few times the fiddle or mandolin takes over for a break. Then the banjo returns with shattering authority, playing a variation halfway up the neck:
CH = choking. See below right

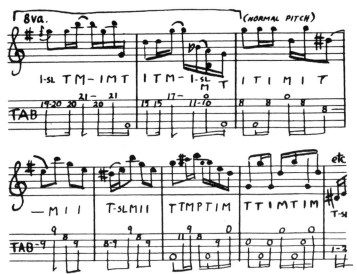

After this tour de force, the banjo returns to normal range; one of the other instruments may take a break, and the piece ends by restating the original theme with a few slight variations. Each banjo picker works out his favorite elaboration of the classic ending "shave and a haircut, two bits". Here is one of Scruggs:

When the letters CH are used above the tablature, they stand for "choking the strings". The finger of the left hand, which is fretting the strings, pushes it to one side, thus raising its pitch. It is a common blues guitar technique. The term probably comes from folk harmonica players, who 'choke up' the instrument with their hands to force a slur out of the reeds. It is impossible with our music notation to describe the actual sound that comes from choking a string. The slur is smooth, and can be more or less exaggerated. The instant the string is plucked it is in motion.

Incidentally, when the strings are higher than their intended pitch, it is very difficult to affect their pitch by choking. When they are more slack than usual, choking is very easy.

Here the 2nd string is fretted at the 10th fret, and then at the same time pushed to one side by the left hand, thus raising it in pitch. A technique much used by blues guitar pickers.

"CHOKING"

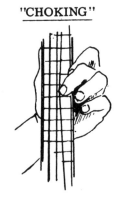

MOLLY AND TENBROOKS

I don't know why I give you the sung melody for this. You ought to hear it. Each verse is sung differently. The song was originally composed in 1878 following a famous Louisville horse race between Kentucky's Ten Broek and California's Miss Mollie McCarthy. Today it is sung in many versions. Some verses stem from an older Irish ballad about the racehorse Skewball. For a detailed writeup, see the Kentucky Folklore Record Vol. II No. 5. Write D. K. Wilgus, W. Kentucky State College, Bowling Green, Ky.

Run, O Molly run,
Run, O Molly run,
Tenbrooks gonna beat you
To the Bright shining sun.
    Bright shining sun, O Lordy
    Bright shining sun.

Tenbrooks was a big bay horse,
He wore that shaggy mane,
He run all around-a Memphis,
He beat the Memphis train.
    Beat the Memphis train, O Lordy,
    Beat the Memphis train.

Tenbrooks said to Molly,
What makes your head so red?
Running in the hot sun,
Puts fever in my head,
    Fever in my head, O Lordy
    Fever in my head.

Molly said to Tenbrooks, you're looking mighty squirrel,
Tenbrooks said to Molly, I'm a-leaving this old world.
    Leaving this old world, O Lordy....etc.

Out in California, where Molly done as she pleased,
Come back to old Kentucky, got beat with all ease. Etc.

The women all a-laughing, the child'n all a-crying,
The men all a-hollering, Old Tenbrooks a-flying. Etc.

See that train a-coming, coming round the curve,
See old Molly running, straining every nerve. Etc.

Kyper, Kyper, you're not riding right.
Molly's beating old Tenbrooks, clear out of sight.

Kyper, Kyper, Kyper, my son,
Give old Tenbrooks the bridle, let old Tenbrooks run.
    Let old Tenbrooks run, O Lordy.. Etc.

Go and catch old Tenbrooks and hitch him in the shade,
They're gonna bury old Molly, in a coffin ready made.
    Coffin ready made, O Lordy... Etc.

FOOTNOTE: Grateful acknowledgement to Michael Seeger for assistance in preparing this chapter.

When one of the other instruments of the band is taking a solo, or when someone is singing, the banjo often "noodles" around up in the highest reaches of the neck, usually on the top three strings. There are a few left hand positions which can be used at various places depending on the chord:

Here is how the first one of the above chords might sound:

Here are two more patterns, slightly different from each other, which use the first four strings very high up:

Most bluegrass bands play songs in G and A, so the banjo would only rarely use the C tuning. The D tuning, however, is quite often used. For this next, tune your banjo ᴀDF#AD.

HARD TIMES

(Transcribed from the playing of Ralph Stanley. Used by permission. © Ralph Stanley)

This piece "Hard Times" is better understood if it is thought of in sections. (A) is introduction. (B) sounds as if it is aimless noodling around, but is an important section in its own right. (C), the minor part, is a "release". (D) is what might be called the main melody. (E) is just a slightly different version of (B), so now go back to 𝄋 and continue through (C) again. Then instead of doing (D) exactly as before, try doing it one octave higher, all the way up the neck.

Check this transcription with their recording, to see how many variations are possible.

THE STANLEY BROTHERS

Ralph Stanley at the left, playing banjo.

Carter Stanley at the right, playing guitar.

Photo by John Cohen

Scruggs invented two special tuning pegs, so that he can change from G tuning to D tuning in the middle of a song. There are several varieties now on the market, but the general principle is pictured below.

A, B, C and D are the standard four tuning pegs.

E and F are the Scruggs pegs.

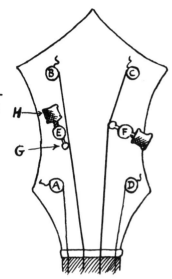

G and H are parts of an adjustable cam. When peg E is given a quarter turn, G presses against the third string, stretching it and raising its pitch. See peg F.

Only the second and third strings are affected. By turning H, G is made to stick out just the right length to stretch the string on the correct new pitch.

You can hear Scruggs use these special pegs on the records of "Earl's Breakdown"; "Foggy Mt. Chimes"; "Randy Lynn Rag" and "Flint Hill Special". Here's the way they are used in the latter:

FLINT HILL SPECIAL

THE NEW LOST CITY RAMBLERS
From left to right: Tom Paley, Mike Seeger, John Cohen

Although bluegrass banjo is best known for being lightning fast, the best performers do a lot of medium tempo numbers as well. But a slow song or one in 3/4 time is rare. To show what can be done, though, here is an old ballad as performed by Sonny Osborne of WWVA, Wheeling, W. Va.

DOWN IN THE WILLOW GARDEN

* Incidentally, in both the above song, and in "Foggy Mountain Breakdown", it is usual for the accompanying instruments to play E major while the banjo plays E minor. It makes a very satisfying discord.

I was once fooling around with a subdued little musical idea and it turned out well enough to record as the opening theme of the Goofing Off Suite. These four measures are repeated over and over:

To them, the following 'tune' (if you can call it that) is whistled:

As in any way of playing the banjo, rhythm is almost of more importance than any single other thing. Until you are sure, crystal-clear sure, don't speed up too fast. Learn how emphasizing different strings gives you control over the syncopation.

Above all, keeping in mind that your **end-all object** is not a shallow show-offishness, learn to integrate all this into the main body of music, so that it says what you want to say.

Earl Scruggs has a page of banjo chords and instructions in the songbook which he and Lester Flatt sell through their radio programs. It can be ordered from P.O. Box 58, Nashville, Tenn.

Photo by John Cohen   Mike Seeger and Earl Scruggs

RECORDINGS OF BLUEGRASS MUSIC

The commercial record companies first became aware in the 1920's that they could make money out of country music. In those days their talent scouts and engineers would set up shop in some city like Knoxville, Tennessee, and advertise "$25 for every song accepted." This seemed like huge money then, and fiddlers, pickers and singers made their way out of the hills and lined up outside their hotel door. Many of these early recordings - collector items now - are fine examples of folk music relatively uninfluenced by the city.

In the 1930's and 40's a new class of professional "country musician" arose, slickly costumed and making a living on the radio and stage. By the 50's the music of some of these sounded so much like the rest of American popular music that they were dubbed "rockabillies". On the other hand Scruggs and some other bluegrass musicians refused to use electrified instruments and represented an attempt to play "the real country way". Even so, **Alan Lomax** has characterized the bluegrass style as 'folkmusic with overdrive'.

Because bluegrass sells well, most of the major companies have bluegrass music in their catalogues. (One small company, Starday, Box 115, Madison, Tenn. specializes in it.) Check the catalogues of Columbia, Decca, Mercury and King and look for such artists as:

Earl Scruggs (especially Col. #1564)
Don Reno and Red Smiley (especially King #552)
Stanley Brothers   Jim Eanes
Stringbean (on Starday)   Hack Johnson
The Osborn Brothers   Jim Martin (Decca)
Bill Monroe   Hylo Brown

As for the smaller companies: Elektra has the Shanty Boys with Roger Sprung, Folkways has "American Banjo Scruggs Style" including numbers by Don Stover, "Mountain Music Bluegrass Style", and the "Country Gentlemen". Atlantic has "Blue Ridge Mountain Music".

Earl Scruggs is still one of the best banjo pickers to learn from, because his playing is extraordinarily clear and even. Many of the numbers are available on 45 rpm as well as 33, which makes them better for learning (you can slow down the record player). Try some of the following titles, all on Columbia.

FOGGY MOUNTAIN JAMBOREE:	FOGGY MOUNTAIN BANJO:
FLINT HILL SPECIAL	GROUND SPEED
SOME OLD DAY	HOME SWEET HOME
EARL'S BREAKDOWN	SALLY ANN
JIMMIE BROWN, THE NEWSBOY	LITTLE DARLIN',
FOGGY MOUNTAIN SPECIAL	REUBEN
IT WON'T BE LONG	CRIPPLE CREEK
SHUCKIN' THE CORN	LONESOME ROAD BLUES
BLUE RIDGE CABIN HOME	JOHN HENRY
RANDY LYNN RAG	FIRE BALL MAIL
YOUR LOVE IS LIKE A FLOWER	SALLY GOODWIN
FOGGY MOUNTAIN CHIMES	BUGLE CALL RAG
REUNION IN HEAVEN	CUMBERLAND GAP

X

OTHER STYLES OF FINGER PICKING

This book does not cover all the many possible ways there are of picking and strumming a banjo. In the books by Billy Faier and by Peggy Seeger (see page 70) you'll find others described. And you, yourself, may discover or invent new patterns and combinations, as you are confronted with new rhythmic problems. Here are a few extra ways of putting the fingers of your right hand to work:

1) This first pattern is one I first saw used by Bascom Lunsford, the country lawyer who for years has run the folk music festival at Asheville, North Carolina. Along with double thumbing and frailing, this was probably one of the most common old time methods of picking the banjo in the mountains.

The index finger not only plucks the melody string, but right afterwards plucks up across the top two or three strings at once (instead of brushing down, as in the basic strum). Lastly, the thumb string kicks off as before. Try it out on this next song - it's an old Child ballad which Lunsford sings beautifully. (You can hear him on the Folkways LP 'Smoky Mountain Ballads')

He tuned his banjo in Mountain Minor: $_G$DGCD.

Bascom Lamar Lunsford

LITTLE MARGET

(Melody to be sung)

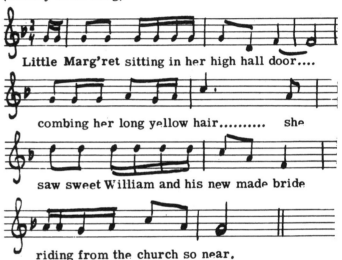

Little Marg'ret sitting in her high hall door....

combing her long yellow hair.......... she

saw sweet William and his new made bride

riding from the church so near.

She throwed down her ivory comb,
She throwed back her long yellow hair,
Said, I'll go down to bid him farewell,
And nevermore go there.
And nevermore go there.

It was all lately in the night,
When they were fast asleep,
Lady Marg'ret appeared all dressed in white,
Standing at their bed feet.

Says, how do you like your pillow, says she,
How do you like your sheet?
And how do you like that gay young lady
Lying in your arms asleep?

Very well do I like my pillow, said he,
Very well do I like my sheet.
But better do I like that fair young lady
Standing at my bed feet.

Once he kissed her lily white hand,
Twice he kissed her cheek,
Three times he kissed her cold corpsy lips
And fell in her arms asleep.

Is little Marg'ret in her room
Or is she in the hall?
No, little Marg'ret's in her cold black coffin
With her pale face to the wall.

And here is the way he played the tune between the verses:

For more banjo music using this style of picking, listen to the Folkways LP of Lunsford, also the LP "Mountain Music Of Kentucky" with Roscoe Holcomb, Bill Cornett, Willie Chapman, and others.

2) A fingerpicking pattern I first found handy for 3/4 time is one my sister Peggy has aptly named "The Lullaby Lick". It's good especially for slow quiet songs for which you want a more sustained effect. Three fingers as well as the thumb are used, plucking each string separately, as in the classic guitar.

I used this for one of my favorite Christmas carols. The words were written by a lawyer in 17th Century France, protesting the selfishness of the rich. Oscar Brand has given it this very good translation:

BURGUNDIAN CAROL

New words and music arrangement by Oscar Brand. Used by permission. ©

And on that night it has been told,
These humble beats so rough and rude,
Throughout the night of holy birth,
Drank no water, ate no food.

How many oxen and donkeys now,
And if they were there when first he came,
How many oxen and donkeys you know
At such a time would do the same?

As soon as to these humble beasts
Appeared our Lord so mild and sweet,
With joy they knelt before his grace,
And gently kissed his tiny feet.

How many oxen and donkeys now,
Dressed in ermine, silk and such,
How many oxen and donkeys you know
At such a time would do as much?

With slight adaptation, the Lullaby Lick is as handy for a slow even accompaniment in 2/4 time. (Complete words for this next song are back on page 9.)

HUSH LITTLE BABY

From the Lomax Collection

For one of my own favorite lullabies, I use a G minor tuning where the 2nd string is lowered one half tone. Result: $G^{DGB\flat D}$. Accompaniment for the first line would go as follows:

Here's the melody to be sung, and the rest of the words. It's a beautiful piece of folk poetry. Think of the generations of slave mothers who made and sang the song while they were tending somebody else's children up in the Big House, thinking of their own children unattended in the slave quarters.

OLD KENTUCKY HOME

by Eastman Johnson, 1859
The New-York Historical Society

ALL THE PRETTY LITTLE HORSES

(Used by permission. From
the collection of John A. and
Alan Lomax.   c 1938)

Chorus: Hush-a-bye, don't you cry,
          Go to sleep, little baby,
          When you awake, you shall have cake
          And all the pretty little horses.

'Way down yonder, down in the meadow,
There's a poor little lambie,
The bees and the butterflies buzzing 'round his eyes,
And the poor little thing cried 'mammy'.

(repeat chorus)

Black and bay, dapple and gray,
Coach and six-a little horses,
When you awake, you'll have cake
And all the pretty little horses.

(repeat chorus)

3) A variation of the Lullaby Lick which I have found
works well for quiet type West Indian songs such as
"The Sloop John B.", and "Choucoune" goes as follows:

(For noisier West Indian songs, try one of the rhumba
rhythms on page 60.)

4) Other examples of finger picking can be found in
two collections of short pieces for the 5-string banjo,
published by Hargail Music Press, 28 W. 38 St. NYC.

One is "Billy Faier's Banjo Book" (Six selections
from a Riverside LP entitled "The Art Of The 5-String
Banjo"); the price is $1.00.

> Three Jolly Rogues of Lynn
> Sailor's Hornpipe
> Hunt the Wren
> Green Corn
> The Dance Of The Spanish Fly
> Irish Medley

The other is "The Goofing - Off Suite", fifteen pieces
from an LP with the same title which I did for Folkways
Records some years ago.   The price is $1.50

> Opening
> Opening Theme (see also this book, page 45.)
> Cindy
> The Girl I Left Behind Me
> All the Pretty Little Horses (this page)
> Anitra's Dance
> Brandy Leave Me Alone
> Jesu, Joy Of Man's Desiring (see page 50)
> O Liza, Poor Gal
> Sourwood Mountain
> Darling Corey (this book, page 22.)
> (Plus three numbers for the guitar and one
> for the mandolin - "Woody's Rag".)

5) Still more can be found in the excellent manual
"The 5-String Banjo - American Folk Styles" by
Peggy Seeger. See page 70).

> In this third edition we have been able
> to correct dozens of mistakes and typo-
> graphical errors which existed in the
> second edition. Don't fail to get a copy
> of the 4th edition, so you can find out
> how many new mistakes have been made!

One disadvantage of this single string work is that it tends to lack the rhythmic accuracy gained when the wrist maintains a free swinging beat. However, you may feel like experimenting along the same lines as the classic guitar. Try the following piece (some will recognize it as a mangled version of an organ part to a Bach chorale).

JESU, JOY OF MAN'S DESIRING

"Correct position to hold the banjo" from Converse's Banjo Tutor, 1892

6) If, when playing a melody with the basic strum, you want to play an alto or tenor part along with it, you can pluck up with two fingers, instead of one. Brush down and thumb the fifth string as before. Here's an example (the Ode to Joy theme from Beethoven's 9th Symphony - remarkable how a good tune can stand up under rough treatment). I find it handiest to pluck up with the ring finger as well as the index finger. You may find the middle finger easier.

ODE TO JOY

7) Once, in admiring the clean spare lines of the music of J.S. Bach, I realized that some of the best blues guitar pickers do the same thing: adhere to a strict economy of notes. So here is an arrangement of an old spiritual in which the banjo purposely plays incomplete chords, and the voice fills in the extra note. I have recorded it on Folkways LP "American Favorite Ballads" Vol. II. The song was taught me by Marion Hicks of Brooklyn, one evening as we sat around the supper table after dishes had been cleared away. She had a deep alto voice, and I have put it in G; if you are a tenor or soprano, you'll have to capo it way up or down.

TWELVE GATES TO THE CITY

G TUNING

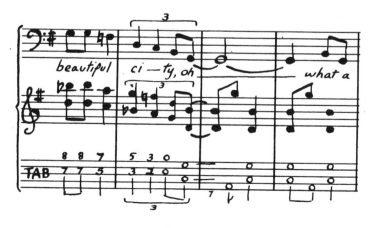

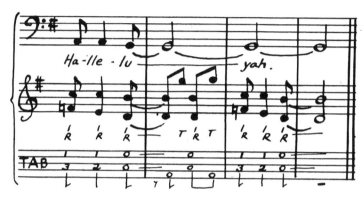

(Complete words and music are in the book "American Favorite Ballads", Oak Pub. 121 W. 47th St. NYC)

8) If you have a very free irregular melody which would be ruined by a metronomic oom-pah-pah accompaniment of any sort, you can try giving a series of fast rolling arpeggios, with the rhythmic outline purposely blurred. I used this in a recording of "Come All Ye Fair and Tender Ladies" and it seemed to work though I am leery of trying it too often. ℵ Means re-

peat the pattern of the previous measure.

COME ALL YE FAIR AND TENDER LADIES

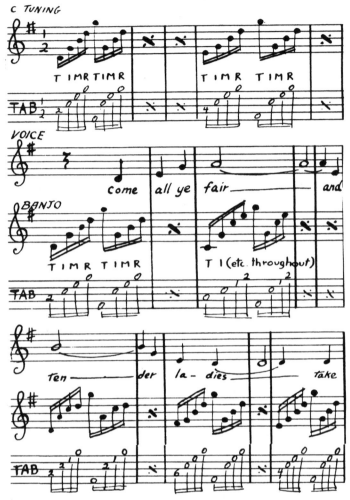

(rest of song can be heard on the Folkways LP "Darling Corey". The words can be found in "English Folksongs In The Southern Appalachians" collected by Cecil Sharpe - your public library should have it)

9) Another possible way of handling this same problem of a free and irregular melody is to do what they do in eastern Europe and Greece - give it a droning bass. Practice your tremolo so it is perfectly even, and try this:

HE LIES IN THE AMERICAN LAND

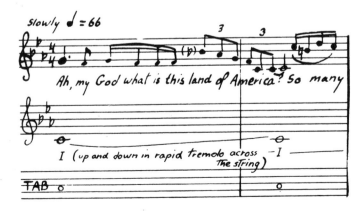

(rest of the song can be heard on Folkways LP "American Industrial Ballads". It was a Slovak - American lament I translated; the original can be found in "Pennsylvania Songs and Legends" edited by George Korson.)

10) Another solution to the problem of a free melody is worth considering: sing it unaccompanied. It's an unorthodox idea nowadays, but not so long ago all the old English and Scottish ballads were sung with no instrumental accompaniment. Freed of entangling alliances, the voice can soar and turn, and accent the irregular rhythms which best bring out the meanings of the words. Peggy Seeger and Ewan MacColl (below) always sing certain songs completely unaccompanied.

Peggy Seeger   Ewan MacColl

XI

WHAMMING
(A Style Of Strumming When You Are In A Crowd And Have To Make A Lot Of Noise)

1) Pick down on the 4th and 5th strings with the back of your middle finger (using a pick).

2) Hammer on or pull off with the left hand.

3) Brush across strings 1,2, and 3, with the back of middle finger. As if shaking your hand off.

4) Brush up across all five strings with the index finger. You'll see this stroke takes the place of the 5th string.

Try this over and over, and your hand should work out an easy roll which should make it possible to play this for a long period of time (dances, etc.).

If the music is slow (swing time, or blues), the above can be modified as follows:

1) Pick down as before on the 4th and 5th strings, with back of middle finger.

2) Again pick down on 4th and 5th strings with back of middle finger.

3) Brush down across strings 1, 2, and 3 as before with back of middle finger.

4) Brush up across all strings with index finger.

You'll find the above strum very handy, because in addition to being fairly loud (a quality you'll need occasionally, believe me) it has a certain amount of subtlety in it, making it far more pleasant to the ears than a straight "bang, bang, bang" down across all strings.

For waltz time, it could be modified as follows:

1) a - Brush down on the 4th and 5th strings with the back of your middle finger.
   b - Hammer on or pull off with the left hand.

2) a - Brush across strings 1, 2, and 3, with the back of middle finger.
   b - Brush up across all five strongs with the index finger.

3) a - (Repeat as in 2a).
   b - (Repeat as in 2b).

HARMONY: "THE CHAIN OF CHORDS"

You may already have discovered that all these various chords you've been playing have a very definite relation to one another. Any song, based in, say the key of C, and using the C chord more often than any other, will nevertheless use the same other chords with it.

There is a reason for this. True, as I pointed out before, much of music is simply illogical tradition, and in other centuries we find other chords much more popular than the ones we use most nowadays. But there is also a very mathematical relationship between all the major chords we use.

For example, what are the chords most closely related to C? Not C♯ or C♭, as you might think, but G, and F. Here's the reason: G is five notes above C, F is five notes below (or 4 above, depending on which direction you count). Since we know that the first harmonic overtone above the octave is a 5th, this looks logical. In other words, one of the first harmonic overtones to a middle C note is a high G.

Now, watch this: If we keep counting up five notes each time, we find that we will name eventually each of the 12 notes in the chromatic scale (white and black keys together), and end right up where we started, at C. I call it the chain of chords, and diagram it like this:

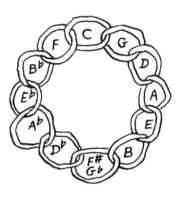

If you will travel around this chain clockwise, you'll perceive that each link is five notes above the previous one. Counter-clockwise, each note is 4 notes above the previous one.

Now, this is important. 85% of the songs we sing, follow this rule: No matter what key a song is in, the other chords used in that song will be mostly in the links right next door. In other words, if you are playing a song in the key of E♭, the chords you'll use mostly will be A♭ and B♭. Musicians have names for these chords. They say that if a song is in, say, D, then D is the Tonic (chord). And the link to the right, A, is the Dominant (chord), and the link to the left, G, is the Subdominant. Thus, in the key of E, E is the tonic, B the dominant, and A the subdominant. You'll find it handy to use these terms.

It is important to remember this, and important, too, to keep referring to this chain of chords until you have memorized it. Because when you start playing songs in keys like B♭, E, and so on, you want to be able to translate the chords I have listed in appendix II, for C, F, G, and D, into the chords you'll need for these new keys. See transposing chart on page 23.

XII

3 MISCELLANEOUS POSTSCRIPTS

If you ever want to play a fast melody alone, with no chords or other accompaniment whatsoever, you can do it with thumb and forefinger. Sometimes the use of another finger will help, and maybe you can get some extra notes by pulling off with the left hand. But try the following, and you will see what I mean:

You'll find it easiest to make a tremolo on the 1st string (or the top two strings together); it's harder to make a tremolo on one of the other strings without sounding nearby strings by mistake. It can be done though. See the cross sectional view sketched below, showing how the index finger plays a tremolo on the 2nd. string, without sounding either the 3rd or 1st strings.

If you ever want to play a tremolo, a nice, steady one can be made with the right index finger, brushing back and forth lightly over a string or two.

Hold the hand as shown. The little finger and the ring finger are braced against the drum. The thumb is braced against the joint of the index finger, high enough so that the latter can move freely.

It's easiest if the index finger doesn't cross the string perpendicularly, but on a slant (the same as that of the right forearm). This makes it less liable for the fingernail to catch on the string.

A roll is a special banjo effect good for ending off a song. Start with all fingers of the right hand doubled up as shown. Then start unwinding the little finger first, next the ring finger, next the middle finger, next the index finger, till the hand looks as shown at bottom. It all happens quite fast. In one "zroomm!" one can make a considerable racket. On a Spanish guitar they call this the "rasgado".

54

XIII

BLUES AND JAZZ

All popular sheet music is printed with the chord names printed above the notes. I think you'll find it best not to bother using your fifth string much with this kind of music, but simply strum right across the other four strings: "zing, zing, zing, zing" since a steady rhythm is usually very necessary for those songs.

For playing the blues, however, there are a number of blues guitar techniques which can easily be transferred to your banjo.

One of them, for example, is the trick of fretting a string a 1/2 tone lower than you are supposed to, and at the same time as you pick it, push it to one side, tightening it until the pitch is slurred up to what it's supposed to be.

Another blues-guitar practice is to put intricate "runs" in between the phrases of a song (in the 'hole' of any blues melody).

To play blues, forget about other methods of strumming, and pluck with the thumb and three fingers of the right hand, as though you were playing a Spanish guitar. Try plunking away at some of the chords exactly as shown here:

Practice this until you have enough rhythmic control to play it three different ways: 1) emphasizing 4th string. 2) emphasizing 5th string. 3) emphasizing top three strings.

One of my favorite blues runs is in the **G** tuning; of course I can't write it down exactly - the essence of any blues is improvisation, and one rarely plays the same blues twice precisely alike. But here is one way:

Important: The 2nd string should be choked (see page *40*) throughout the first measure, then released in the second measure. In the third measure the choke goes on and off alternately. The 3rd string is choked in the tenth measure.

HARMONY LESSON: BLUES HARMONY

95% of all blues have the same basic harmony, which is why it is so much fun to play blues in a jam session...makes it easier to stay together. Blues may be fast or slow, high or low, and there may be many subtle variations within this framework, but if you will study the following, it will be easy for you to pick up any blues.

The average "three line" blues has 12 bars.

The first line of the verse is sung to the first four bars, and is all in the tonic chord, possibly ending with an added 7th note.

The repeat of the first line takes up the next four bars, the first two of which are in the <u>sub-dominant</u> with an added 7th and/or 9th), and the last two of which return to the tonic.

The last line of the blues takes up the last four bars, the first two of which go into the **dominant**, and the last two of which return to the tonic.

In diagram form it would look like this:

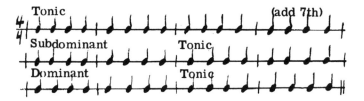

If you'll examine the example of blues given on the previous page, you'll see this applies. Try it for a verse of "Easy Rider Blues".

EASY RIDER BLUES

G G^7
Easy rider, see what you done done...(Lord, Lord)

C   G
Easy rider, see what you done done...................

D^7 G
You made me love you; now your man done come..

1) Sometimes the words of the verse take up the first two lines, and the 3rd line, always repeated, becomes the refrain. Such is "Frankie and Johnny", "Boll Weevil", and "Stagolee".

2) Sometimes you get a "4-line blues". Usually this means the middle line, which goes into the sub-dominant, is repeated. Occasionally though, it will be the first or last line which has been repeated. And there are many other variants. 'Easy Rider' is often a 4-line blues. So also is 'Git Back Blues' (see Kolb, Treasury of Folk Songs.) 'Going Down The Road Feeling Bad', though not usually thought of as a blues, appears to have at least started off as one, when you examine its harmonic pattern.

3) Sometimes the first line is crowded with the words of a verse, and the 2nd and 3rd lines repeat always as a chorus, like this:

BOTTLE UP AND GO

O the little banty rooster and the dominicker hen

They run around together but they ain't no kin

CHORUS

You got to bottle up and go......   You got to

bottle up and go. All you high powered women

sure got to bottle up and go!

(The extra chords in the last two lines are typical variations.)

The above song can be heard powerfully sung by Leadbelly on Folkways Records. Another fine blues which Leadbelly sang (and Big Bill Broonzy has a record of it also) is "In The Evening When The Sun Goes Down", written by the late Leroy Carr. Here's

The Tarriers: Bob Carey, Clarence Cooper, and Eric Weissberg.   Photo by David Gahr.

a run I often put between the verses when singing it
The first two measures are just introduction。

IN THE EVENING WHEN THE SUN GOES DOWN

Leeds Music Inc。 Used by permission

Banjo Player   By Thomas Eakins

BLUES RHYTHM

Another thing to notice about the blues is that the rhythm is nearly always 4/4, whether fast or slow. But especially when a blues is slow, you'll hear a quarter note frequently split up into triplets, and then if you'll listen carefully you'll see that all blues and jazz rhythm has more of a 12/8 rhythm feeling, than straight 4/4.

Listen to some blues records, and you'll know what I mean. I imagine the triplet feeling comes because the downbeats are emphasized so strongly.

The arrows point to the four downbeats in each measure.

Thus each of the notes, instead of being equal in length, tend to sound more like this.

So it is natural to break into this:

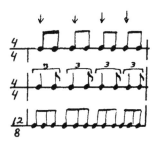

The last three measures are about the same as in the blues piece on the previous page. I told you that I really know only one way to play the blues. Slow, fast or in different keys。

> Let music sound while he doth
>   make his choice ;
> Then, if he lose, he makes a swan-
>   like end,
> Fading in music.
>   "Merchant of Venice,"
>   Act III。, Scene 2.

Woody Guthrie

BLUES SCALES

Remember, also, that the blues characteristically tend to flatten the 3rds and 7ths of the scale, and occasionally sharpen the 4ths. Furthermore, dissonances are more the rule that the exception. This is most common when you will sing a minor third and play a major third on the instrument.

Of course, as I said before, there are many different varieties of blues. It might be best to look further into this magnificent modern song form. Like the sonnet or the limerick, it is a form, a vehicle for a 1000 and one varieties.

Don't think that you can just follow these directions mechanically and sing the blues. Without the subtle and characteristic inflections of both voice and instrument, without the traditional phraseology of melody, and the "answering back" of the improvised runs at the end of the lines, you haven't got it all.

Your best bet is to try and locate a blues guitar picker living near you. It should't be hard, if you live in the USA. Lacking someone to watch closely and play with, get hold of the blues recordings by such as:

Blind Lemon Jefferson
Lonnie Johnson
Leadbelly
Brownie McGhee
Big Bill Broonzy
Josh White
Bessie Smith
John Lee Hooker
Lightnin Hopkins
Memphis Slim

The old 78 rpm records may be unobtainable, but some of the small independent labels have reissued them on LPs.

Also get hold of a copy of "Folk Blues" by Jerry Silverman (Macmillan, NYC)

CAN A MUSICIAN BE TRI-LINGUAL?

The good folk musician is a creator as well as a re-creator, and when he creates, to make solid sense, he should "improvise within the idiom". Otherwise he may be like the scholar who sprinkles his work with phrases in a foreign language - he knows what he means, but nobody else does. There is always the need for experimentation, but don't expect people to want to listen to it - anymore than the experimental cook would expect people to eat his avant garde concoctions. He might be Expressing Himself, but the stomach might not agree.

It is natural for a folk musician to prefer to make all his music within one idiom. It is like a writer doing all of his writing in one language. G.B. Shaw once said that it was impossible for a man to be a really good writer in more than one language. The brain could not get all geared up for one syntax and vocabulary if it was being distracted and confused by another.

Some musicians, therefore, who try to pretend that they are equally familiar with many idioms may end up sounding like a perpetual tourist who has a dilettante's knowledge of many parts of the world, but does not know his own home.

> Of course, if you really want to play a lot of blues, you will probably want to do it on a steel stringed guitar anyway. The notes are sustained longer; less plunky. This chapter is really written for the banjo picker who finds himself in the company of some bluesy guitar pickers. Or boozy ones.

SONNY TERRY   Photo by David Gahr

58

XIV

SPANISH AND SOUTH AMERICAN MUSIC

...is not hard to play on the banjo. You may find you want to abandon the square dance strum occasionally, though, and as with the blues, finger each string separately. Here's one run which is very characteristic of Spanish Flamenco (gypsy) guitar music:

Notice in the above that while the thumb plays a kind of melody, the index and middle fingers incessantly but lightly touch the 1st string. Practice it until it becomes exceedingly fast and smooth. Arch the right wrist slightly for better control. The first string is plucked up, of course.

Listen to some Flamenco recordings (Montoya, Escudero, Sabicas or Gomez) to see how runs such as the above are worked into a song.

In the album "Songs Of The Lincoln Battalion" I played three such Spanish melodies on the banjo.

One of these is still almost my favorite song. Although I know I don't pronounce the words exactly right, I hope I can always sing it in honor of those brave men who volunteered to fight Hitler and Mussolini a few years before it was popular to do so. Here, in my hillbilly flamenco, are the notes for the opening introductory verse:

VIVA LA QUINCE BRIGADA

You'll note there is a very characteristic harmony which will end a song even on a dominant chord, **and** using over and over such chords progressions as: Cm, B♭, A♭, G.

<u>Rhumba rhythm</u> also sounds good on a banjo; here are two ways to get it:

➤ 1) Brush down across all strings with the back of middle finger.
2) Brush down across all strings with thumb (if you want, just 5th string)
3) Brush <u>up</u> across all strings with index finger
▷ 4) Brush down across all strings with back of middle finger
5) Brush down as before again with thumb
6) Brush <u>up</u> across strings again with index finger
▷ 7) Brush down again with back of middle finger
8) Brush up again with index finger

...and do the above over and over again till it goes smoothly. The accents should be where the arrows point. This irregularity is the basis of the rhumba rhythm.

Here's another way of getting a rhumba rhythm - better but harder:

➤ 1) Pick down on the 4th and 5th strings with the back of the middle finger, and /or hammer down with the left hand on some chord at the same time.

2) A "roll"; ruffle your right hand down across
3) all strings, each finger successively straightening out.

▷ 4) With the thumb, pluck the 5th string, and at the same time hammer down again with the fingers of the left hand.

5) Brush lightly <u>up</u> across 1st and 2nd strings with index finger

6) Brush lightly <u>down</u> across strings 1,2, and 3, with the back of the ring finger and little finger.

▷ 7) Again thumb the 5th string, at the same time hammering down with the left hand.

8) Brush lightly <u>up</u> across strings 1 and 2 with the index finger.

The above is really quite tricky and subtle rhythm, and will take some repetition to go smoothly. If you have not already noticed, I'll point out that a rhumba rhythm is essentially a 4/4 time broken up into eight pieces, with the accents syncopated thus: <u>123</u> <u>123</u> <u>12</u>.

In South America they have, of course, many, many other fascinating rhythms. You can learn them from a good guitar player and transfer his technique to the banjo. Wish I knew more myself, along this line!

The second of the two rumba strums given at the left can be adapted quite easily for square dancing. There should be other instruments besides the banjo in the ensemble, to maintain the basic beat. With practice you can vary the rhythmic emphasis.

Banjonalities (The Freemasonry of Art)
By G. Du Maurier, 1890's

He: "I beg your pardon - but - er - would you be so kind as to give me the 'G'?"
She: "Oh, certainly." (Gives it.)
He: "Thanks awfully!"(Bows and proceeds on his way.)

XV

SUMMARY

As you have by now gathered, I have *usually* not tried to
teach you in this manual any exact method of playing
any particular song, but have only briefly outlined
many different methods by which you can improvise
your own accompaniment to any song you want to
sing. From here on, you're on your own.

While you may have found the written notes valu-
able to learn from, I hope you will not be too depen-
dent on them, but will rather try to develop your ear
and your imagination. At present there is practically no written music for the 5-string banjo available. When learning a song from a book, you will
have to translate the melody and the chord markings
to your own style of playing.

It is easy to get bored with a song if you just
plunk it out, chord after chord. If you try working
out such things as counter-melodies, and bass runs,
however, you'll find it starts to sparkle. And the
banjo is so wonderfully adapted to sparkling - a com-
monplace melody becomes quite subtle when surrounded with many other notes. Then it becomes
like trying to pick out a constellation from all the
other glittering stars in the sky.

Then when you play with other instruments, such
as piano, guitar, mandolin, fiddle, harmonica, re-
corder, etc. you find additional enjoyment from taking the low part while they take the high part, or vice
versa, and from taking the melody while they take
the chords, or vice versa. Your music can become
a wonderfully creative experience.

The people I learned banjo from were mostly old
farmers, miners, or working people of one trade or
another, who had played the instrument during their
courting days, and later kept it hanging on the wall
to pass away the time of an evening. Often they knew
only a few tunes apiece, and maybe only one method
of strumming, which they had picked up from their
father, or a neighbor. Yet what they knew, they knew
well, and the simple, rippling rhythm of their banjo
had more art in it than many a hectic performance
piece by a professional virtuoso.

What I am aiming at saying is, that it is better to
know a few things well than attempt something
flashy which sounds sloppy or grating. The tenor
banjo was ruined, really, by exhibitionists who made
an athletic exhibition out of each performance; after
the piece was over the audience was amazed, of
course, as at the circus, but it was not music which
moved or delighted one.

I rather think that as more Americans take hold
again of their traditions of folkmusic, and as we become acquainted with many different kinds of songs
from various corners of the world, this 5-string banjo is liable to develop as never before. Not only will
we be playing the old ballads and breakdown, but
music from Europe, Israel, Russia, Asia, Africa, and
South America. And the unique qualities of this instrument, with its penetrating needle-points of sound,
will be heard in many new forms.

APPENDIX 1

IF YOU HAVE NEVER BEFORE PLAYED A BANJO.. look for the following things in buying one, or taking care of it.

The P E G S may be of several different types but in all cases should be firm and tight to hold the string yet free of rust, etc., and able to turn accurately and smoothly. Mechanical pegs can usually be tightened or loosened by turning a screw. Oil them, if necessary.

In buying S T R I N G S, be sure to ask for "5-string banjo strings", not those for a Tenor banjo. Get a set with an unwound 3rd string. Black Diamond is the most common make. John D'Angelico, 37 Kenmare St. NYC, sells extra long strings for banjos with lengthened necks - and the winding on his 4th string really lasts. $1.25 a set. See p. 51 for nylon strings.

When putting on strings, allow an inch or so extra to wrap around the peg. Break off what is left over by making a kink in the wire; then a strong yank will part it.

The strings should be about 1/8 to 3/16 " high off the fingerboard at the 12th fret. If they are much higher the strings will be stretched out of tune when you press them to the frets. You should contrive to either lower your bridge, or to bend the banjo neck back by inserting a small strip of wood at the point marked "A".

If the strings are too low, they will buzz and you had best heighten your bridge.

In damp weather or living near salt water, rub oil on the strings to keep them from rusting. Old strings have poor tone and pitch and may need to be replaced.

Incidentally, a 1st string can be substituted for a 5th string if you wish; they are of approximately the same diameter wire.

In order to play in different keys, you will need a banjo C A P O. See Lesson VI, p. 23.

The F R E T S must all be firmly laid in the fingerboard, rounded slightly on the top, so the finger can slide up and down the string without catching. While some old fashioned banjoes had no frets at all, you will need them; they should be no more than 1/32" high. And if any of them is a little too high or low, you will find it necessary to adjust or replace it, for the strings will buzz. Or else you will find yourself skipping a note when playing. A simple test is to play a chromatic scale on each string, to see if all frets are correct.

One of the common defects of a second hand banjo is a W A R P E D F I N G E R B O A R D. Lay a yardstick or other straight edge along it or sight along it carefully. More than 1/10 of an inch sag and the instrument will be too out of pitch to bother using.

It is of utmost importance that the D R U M be tight enough to give a good tone. Of course, if the skin is old it may break if tightened too much, so be careful. However, a good new drum head will stand being tightened until the pressure of the strings will not depress the bridge more than 1/16 of an inch. In damp air you will have to tighten the head; be sure to loosen it again, though, before dry weather cracks it.

A K E Y or wrench, is needed to turn the bracket nuts, thus tightening the drum.

The B R I D G E should be placed so that when you fret any string at the 12th fret, you get a tone <u>exactly</u> one octave higher than the string's open <u>unfretted</u> tone. With old strings you may need to slant the bridge slightly to make it accurate for the 2nd, 3rd, and 4th strings.

A drop of Elmer's Glue on the edge of the bridge helps to keep it from sliding. A deepened notch for the 5th string if your thumb is catching the 5th string too hard.

An A R M R E S T, besides being more comfortable, prevents summertime perspiration from rotting the edge of the drum head.

One item not pictured here is a cloth to stuff inside the drum when you want to play without being too loud. A handkerchief is too small, a bath towel too big but a D I A P E R is just right.

Myself, I like to attach a S H O U L D E R S T R A P at points A and B. Then if I wish, I can sling the whole thing upside down behind my right shoulder to walk down the street.

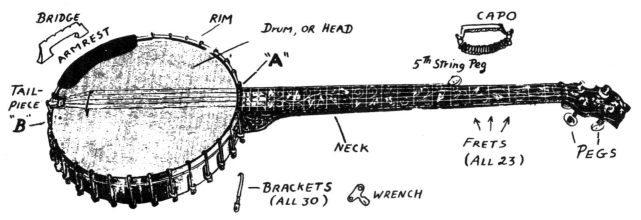

APPENDIX 2

WHERE TO BUY A BANJO

Second hand banjoes are nowhere so easy to find as they were when this manual was first written thirteen years ago. Nevertheless, since a wellmade musical instrument, well cared for, will not wear out in three years like a Detroit car, hard searching will often uncover a fine banjo for a very low price, either in a pawnshop, an auction or someone's attic. If you locate a banjo with a really fine and solid rim but a warped old neck, it might be worth it to have a new neck made to fit it. Can be done.

A new banjo, like any good instrument, is liable to be expensive. But don't make the mistake of thinking that you can automatically make better music on a more expensive instrument. Some of the best banjo picking I ever heard in my life was done on the cheapest mail-order banjoes. Both Sears Roebuck and Monky Ward carry them. Prices on banjoes start around $30 and go up to several hundred dollars. Companies making them now in the USA include Kay, Harmony, Gretsch, Gibson and Vega. The latter custom builds **a long necked model, as does also a new little compa-ny in Boulder, Colorado (the ODE** Company Jamestown Star Route, Boulder, Colorado). The latter, like any reputable firm, will guarantee a neck against any possible warping.

If you know anyone traveling to Europe and back, good 5-string banjoes are manufactured in both West Germany and England. In London see Clifford Essex Ltd., 8 New Compton St. W. C. 21,. European banjoes put their 5th string peg at the tip end of the neck, in the center of the other four. The 5 string ducks into a hole at the 5th fret, goes through a small tube, and emerges just beyond the nut.

Bluegrass banjo pickers prefer using a resonator on the bank of the instrument. At the other extreme, some players prefer a lightweight wooden rim, no frets and nylon strings to get that old 'plunky' tone. You will have to decide for yourself which you like best.

Some companies also now sell you a banjo with Scruggs pegs already on it (see page 44 for a description.)

HOW TO LENGTHEN THE NECK

If your 5-string banjo is of the usual kind, the 5th string peg will stick out between the 4th and 5th frets (Look again at the diagram, page 34). This has certain disadvantages. For one thing, if you want to play in the key of G♭(F♯) you cannot move your capo high enough for it.

Furthermore, if you want to use a C tuning to accompany some song, but the key of C is too high for your voice (you may prefer B♭) you are also stuck. The only way you can get B♭ is in the G tuning, three frets up.

Therefore, I have found it very convenient to do a little carpentry on my banjo neck, lengthening it by two frets. Thus I can play in F or B♭ without having to capo so far up the neck that I lose my bass notes.

Shown here is one method of sawing the neck off, and with good glue and dowels, making the lengthened end hold firm. (Cheaper and easier than trying to carve a complete new neck).

Don't attempt this yourself, of course, unless you are sure of your ability; a professional repairman would charge $20-$60 for such a job. In addition to gluing an iron-firm joint, you must place the new frets in exactly the right position. The distance from the bridge to a new fret should be twice the distance from the bridge to its 'octave fret'.
This assumes the bridge to be in a mathematically correct position. You can place it there by measuring the distance from the old nut to the 12th fret. Exactly double the distance, and you have the correct location for the bridge.

<u>NO MATTER WHAT BANJO YOU HAVE</u> there is one small adjustment you'll want to make: a small screw placed in the fingerboard above the 5th string. Here's the reason for it.

In order to play the keys of E and E♭ (C tuning) and B♭ , B (G tuning) you'll have to tighten your 5th string, raising it's pitch the same amount that you raise that of the other strings with the capo. . . this is almost impossible to do without breaking the 5th string. I therefore put a small round-headed screw in the fingerboard, 5 frets above the 5th string peg, and directly under the 5th string itself. Don't screw it down tight, but leave about 1/32'' clearance under the head; then you can slip the fifth string under it, thus artificially fretting it. In this new position you can hit the higher pitch you need. If, for any reason, you want to experiment with other screws still higher on the fingerboard, of course that is possible too.

Since the above was written, a number of people have experimented with making "5th string capo". They are not manufactured as yet, but you might try devising one yourself. One of the most successful one's I've seen was made by songwriter Ernie Marrs. A small piece of old clock spring is heated and bent to this shape. The top hold the 5th string down. The lower end hooks into a narrow groove dug in the back of the neck, exactly parallel to the edge of the fingerboard.

ON THE SUBJECT OF BANJO CASES

Under the hard usage of traveling, the average instrument case starts coming to pieces in a few years. I finally made my own case out of waterproof plywood with steel guard corners. My brother, Mike, made a similar one, shaped slightly like a child's coffin, which he solemnly decorated with a large black cross.

These homemade jobs turned out to be pretty heavy, though, and about four years ago I designed a padded leatherette banjo case, closed with a zipper, and slung on the shoulder. My long suffering wife, Toshi, sewed it up for me, and it worked out so well that I am proud to pass on the design to anyone who'd like to use it or improve upon it.

The key to its success is an inner sling, which carried the whole weight. Otherwise the seams on the lower end would split in no time.

How it is carried:

The banjo and guitar cases made by Blue Heron in Carlota, CA. never split their seams, I use them now.
May 2012

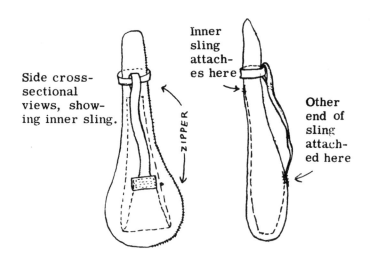

The big advantage of such a case, in my view, is the ease of carrying, leaving one's hands free for opening doors, carrying suitcases, etc. Because it is always nearby, in plane, train, or car, the instrument actually gets more careful handling than it would from the usual baggage departments.

In cutting the pattern, make sure you not only make it large enough for side panels, seams, etc. but also leave a little extra room for spare shirts, socks, papers, whistles, and apples, cheese or pastrami sandwiches.

APPENDIX 3

CHORDS! CHORDS! CHORDS!

On the opposite page are listed more chords than any sensible person could conceivably use. (Do not attempt to memorize. For reference only) Yet what you see here is by no means all of the possible chord combinations. You are shown several different ways to make each chord. The first is the usual one down nearest the nut. You'll have to figure out for yourself the best way to maneuver the fingers of your left hand to the positions shown by those black dots. Often one finger will have to "barre" across several strings.. (such as $A^\flat$ in the upper left hand corner)..

Remember these chords are mainly for use when you play a song in the key of C. If you play a song in any other key I advise you to use a capo and learn to transpose (see transposing chart, page 23).

With a capo, you can use the C tuning to play in $D^\flat$, D, $E^\flat$, E and F. If you have a long necked banjo you can also play in B, $B^\flat$, and A - or lower, if you want to tune all your strings slack. With a capo and in the G tuning, you can play in $A^\flat$, A, $B^\flat$, B and C. With a long necked banjo you can move the capo down and play in $G^\flat$, F, and E.

Normally the 5th string is not fretted. With a C or G chord and with a few other chords, it sounds okay. Its use is indicated by a small Roman numeral V. Where this sign is lacking, it means that the 5th string may clash with the chord and you had best not sound it; so strum so that just the first four strings are heard.

To locate a chord for a certain key, read horizontally from the left. To pinpoint the kind of chord (i.e. a minor chord) read vertically down from from the top. Thus a $B^{\flat 7}$ chord would be found in the third row down, and in the fourth and fifth row from the left:

The number to the right means Fret (counting up from the Nut)

By "Major 7th chord" is meant, a 1-3-5-7- chord (i.e. $G-B-D-F^\sharp$) in any combination.
"Major 6th chord" means 1-3-5-6 (G-B-D-E).
"9th chord" means 1-3-5-7-9 ($G-B-D-F^\sharp-A$).
Minor chords simply have a flatted third.
"Minor 7th" chords mean add the 7th ($G-B^\flat-F^\sharp$).
"Minor 6th" means add the 6th.
An augmented chord raises the 5th a half tone, ($G-B-D^\sharp$).
A diminished chord lowers the third and the fifth a half tone ($G-B^\flat-D^\flat$).

con't on page 66

CHORD POSITIONS FOR THE C TUNING : GCGBD

CHORD POSITIONS FOR THE G TUNING: (G) DGBD USE UP OR DOWN THE NECK

CHORD POSITIONS FOR THE D TUNING: (A) DF#AD USE UP OR DOWN THE NECK

CHORDS FOR THE G TUNING

...are the same as for the C tuning except for the 4th string. If your fingers can't reach further down along the neck, you'll have to find the right new place. Thus:

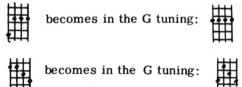

Incidentally, remember that every time you fret a string on the 12th fret, you get almost the same chord (and sometimes a better one) by just lifting your finger and playing that string open, an octave lower. Test out this principle with some of the chords you see on the previous page.

Similarly, any chord position that does not include open strings can be repeated 12 frets higher up the neck. You'll notice that in all these 240 chords there are only a few main positions. You just use them higher or lower on the neck.

OTHER TUNINGS

For chord positions in other tunings, we can only advise you to use your own ingenuity. In this book, variant tunings are mentioned on the following pages:

Variant G tunings: $_G$DGCD ("Mountain Minor") pages 36 and 46. $_G$DGAD see page 32. $_G$DGB♭D see page 49. $_E$DGBD see page 37. If you can get your fifth string a full octave higher than the first string, you might try the song "Green Corn" in this tuning: $_D$DGBD.

There are also variants of the C tuning, such as $_C$CGBD, $_G$CGAD, $_G$CGCD, $_G$CGCE.

Two variants of the D tuning are given in this book: $_{F♯}$DF♯AD (page 21) and $_A$DF♯AD (page 42). You might like to look into others, such as $_A$BEAD, which Mike Seeger says is fine for the song "Cumberland Gap".

A hundred years ago the gut strings of banjoes were tuned a minor third lower than steel strings are nowadays. Even so, some players like to tune their instruments still higher, to get a more ringing tone out of it. Grandpa Jones, for example, usually tunes his instrument $_A$EAC#E - that is, one whole tone higher than the normal G tuning. However, it is hard to choke the strings when they are this tight. Rufus Crisp of Allen, Ky., who never used a capo, used some eighteen tunings. Here are a few of them which we haven't already mentioned: $_G$GGBD, $_G$FGBD, $_F$CFAC, $_{F♯}$ADAD, $_{F♯}$GEAD, $_G$GDAD. $_G$DGDE

APPENDIX 4

HOW TO READ MUSIC - SLIGHTLY

If you don't already know how to read music, you might take a gander at this page. It is really very simple - like touch typing, a matter of learning a few simple things well. Though you may never be so proficient as to be able to pick up a concerto and read it at sight, if you learn enough to pick out a tune in a songbook, you'll find it of much help..

First, most melodies are written in the "treble clef". This means that you will see a spiral thingummy at the left end of the staves; it circles a line which represents a G note, as you see below. Here are two scales in the key of "C" (they start and end on C).

A "sharp" sign (♯) preceding any note raises its pitch a half tone. A "flat" sign (♭) lowers it a half a tone. Thus when a song is in some other key than C, and you "have to start playing on the black notes", these "black notes" will be pointed out by putting the appropriate sharps or flats at the beginning of a song. Below are some of the most common of these "key signatures".

If at any time you want to go back, say, from F♯ to ordinary F ("F natural"), you put a "natural" sign (♮) in front of the note.

<u>Now go through any songbook and pick out melodies you already know, and try following the notes up and down.</u>

Second, the rhythm of a song is marked by "measures", signified by vertical bars across the staff, as shown below. Within a measure there may be several beats; the most common rhythms are known as 2/4 (two quarter notes per measure), 3/4, 4/4, and 6/8 (six eighth notes per measure).

A whole note (O) is the longest note (equal to four beats). For anything longer than that you tie two notes together, thus : O͡O . A dot right after a note increases its length by 1/2. Thus, all measures below have four beats in them (including "rests" - the noise stops but the rhythm keeps going!). Use your arithmetic to see if each measure totals four beats. In one measure I purposely goof.

The following sign over a note > means you should accent, or emphasize it.

A double bar is put at the end of a song, or a section within a song.

Two dots in front of it means go back and repeat from the beginning, or go back to the previous double bar, where you will see two similar dots. Over this double bar you'll sometimes see a fancy little cross. The letters D.S. over the last double bar stand for the Italian words "Dal Segno" meaning "from the sign".

This sign: 𝄍 means "repeat the previous measure". If there is a number over it, it means to repeat the previous measure a certain number of times.

Now here is a tricky bit: often when you repeat a musical phrase, the last measure will have over it a long horizontal line with the letter 1. Right after the double bar will be a similar line with the letter 2. On repeating the phrase, (because the double bar with dots told you to) when you come to the "1. " - skip it and go right ahead to "2. ". In other words, the same phrase has two different endings. See page **59**.

The above rudiments are only a start; any music store has manuals which will teach you the meaning of dozens of other hieroglyphics and Italian terms which it will help you to know. The best way for you to learn, though, is to go through songbook after songbook, checking your knowledge first with songs you know, and then trying to decipher unfamiliar melodies.

TABLATURE AS USED IN THIS BOOK

...uses the same vertical bars to divide the music into measures of two, three or four beats. And the repeat signs are also the same.

Each beat can then be broken up into shorter notes, with little tails, dots etc., just as in regular music writing.

The five lines of the tablature represent the five strings of the banjo, with the 5th string at the bottom. The numbers refer to the fret at which the left hand stops the string. "O" means "open string - not fretted at all". See page 7.

The fingering indication above the tablature refers to how the string is sounded:

T = right thumb, plucking down
I = right index finger, nearly always plucking up. (For exception, see page 46).
M = middle finger, plucking up, unless you are frailing (see page 29) when it means the back of the middle (or index) fingernail, plucking down.
R = ring finger, plucking up, (see page 7).
B = brushing down across all or several strings (see page 7).
H = hammering on (see page 14).
P = pulling off (see page 16).
SL = slide (see page 30).
CH = choke (see page 40).
E or F = Scruggs pegs (see page 44).

"Can you read music?"

"Not enough to hurt my playing."

APPENDIX 5

FINGERNAILS

In case you haven't noticed already, its of utmost importance that the fingernails of each hand be the right length.

Those of the left hand will have to be short, so the finger can come down directly and firmly on the string, without the nail touching at all.

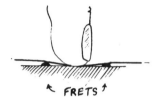

← FRETS →

Those on the right hand should be neither too long or too short. When plucking, the flesh of the fingertip should touch the string first, but the nail be last to leave it. And when picking down, only the nail should touch the string.

Unless you have unusually tough fingernails, you'll have to wear fingerpicks on your right whenever you play long or loud. Cumbersome as they are at first, and too loud for home use, they will nevertheless protect your nails from wearing thin at the edge, or tearing.

Hardly any two people use the same kind of picks. The kind I like are metal, and look like this (left):

Bend one slightly and put it on the index finger, thus (for plucking up):

Straighten out another pick slightly and put it on the middle finger. I find that thus I can use it both for frailing (picking down) and for 3-finger picking (plucking up). If this doesn't work for you, you may want to make your own fingerpicks.

I also use a fingerpick to protect the nail on the ring finger when brushing down. Here you can use the celluloid kind, if you wish.

I don't usually use a thumbpick because for the kind of singing I do they are too loud. But if you play with a string band, you're liable to need that piercing volume. Bluegrass musicians mostly use thumbpicks, and just two finger picks, both facing the same direction. (up).

You needn't worry about a pick for the little finger - not used enough.

At left—
Egyptian girl musician with instrument slung by a belt.

At Right—
Egyptian girl dancing while playing.

(Reproduced from Paintings found in a Tomb in Ancient Thebes.)

✳ Footnote To History

(Continuing the subject from page 5).

The historically minded might like to pursue this matter further. Consider these points:

1) Thomas Jefferson, in his 'Notes on Virginia' (1782) mentions the "banjar" as being the chief instrument of American Negroes.

2) The instrument is mainly known in Africa in the northern half, the area of Moslem influence. (The slave trade was most intensive along the west coast of Africa.

3) The American folk style of playing seems to me to be basically African. A subtle rhythmic-melodic pattern is set up which repeats itself with no change in tempo, no matter what complex variations may be introduced. The sung melody may be quite free, at the same time. One can see a parallel in the playing of boogie-woogie piano.

4) Throughout all of the Near East and Far East instruments like the banjo are common. While they might have independently developed on two continents, one is tempted to believe that there was some direct connection. Two instruments in India have short strings played by the thumb, just like the banjo. One is the sitar (cousin of the guitar) and the other is known as the sarod - and has a drumskin head! Archeologists tell us that the ancient Egyptians had orchestras of 600 instruments, and some of them were plucked, and had skin-topped sounding boxes. Who learned what and with which and from whom? We will probably never know the exact prehistory of the instrument.

5) Paul Cadwell, New York Lawyer, and friend to all banjoists, quotes a Judge Farrar of Virginia, who learned banjo from Sweeney in the 1840's, "I am confident that Sweeney added the bass string." in other words, it would now appear likely that the use of a higher pitched thumb string was pre-Sweeney after all.

Above: 'The Banjo Player' by Wm. S. Mount, 1856.

Below, an instrument played by present day minstrels in a village 100 miles east of Dakar, West Africa. The strings, of unequal length, are held by friction of a simple loop.

Below: a four stringed gourd banjo, about 1800.

Above: Joel Walker Sweeney, 1810-1860. The daguerreotype is from an interesting article in the Spring 1949 Quarterly of the Los Angeles County Museum. Below: a banjo made by Sweeney for his niece, who was left-handed. It had six brackets and no frets. The 5th string peg protruded vertically through the neck.

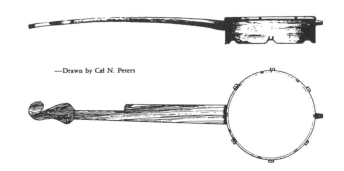

—Drawn by Cal N. Peters

'Modern Music' from Goday's Magazine, 1861.

"The Old Plantation"—water color, about 1800.
—In the Ludwell-Paradise House at Williamsburg, Virginia.

APPENDIX 6

BOOKS ON THE 5-STRING BANJO

For some years this little manual was the only publication in its field. Now, I'm glad to say, it's not alone. There's Billy Faier's carefully notated collection of banjo pieces (see p. 49). Grandpa Jones had a banjo instruction book specializing in frailing, but he has moved, and I haven't located his new address yet. Earl Scruggs puts a page of instructions in his songbook (see p. 45). Best of all is the following:

"The 5-String Banjo: American Folk Styles" by Peggy Seeger, 52 pages, $1.95 Hargail Music Press, 28 W. 38 St. N.Y.C. My sister wrote it when she first went to England and was besieged with requests for information. Lest I be accused of family pride, I reprint parts of two reviews of the book:

> So when Peggy, our closest approximation to a Compleat City Folksinger, pours her knowledge of banjo lore into a manual; it is just cause for every picker to run (not walk) to his nearest music store and grab a copy. The first

> The basic value of Peggy's book is its documentation of the myriad of styles she has learned from others or worked out herself from her thorough knowledge of classical and folk music. For

> it; Peggy seems to be writing on the assumption that there exist serious folk musicians who want to learn a lot of the complexities of the instrument. The

J. Pancake and P. Nelson in Little Sandy Review.

Since there is only one other widely-available banjo instruction book, HOW TO PLAY THE FIVE STRING BANJO, by Peter Seeger, some comparisons might be helpful. Peter includes only a few songs but writes out, in tablature, at least part of the way they may sound as solo banjo pieces. (In my experience, some people find the use of tablature extremely helpful; others have great difficulty in learning to read it.) Peggy, as already pointed out, includes no instrumental transcriptions, but prints many more songs, twenty-seven in all, with complete texts. In a book of over-all excellence, this is one of the nicest parts; she has selected a wide variety of fresh, unhackneyed tunes, both slow and fast, familiar and unusual, and all of them fun to play. Peggy also goes into the question of harmony and chord progressions more thoroughly than does Peter; he, on the other hand, includes a partial discography (very important for banjo players), a section on how to choose and care for the banjo, and some interesting historical data. In other words, both books are useful in their own ways; both supplement each other nicely. There need be no schism in the Seeger family.

In sum, then, THE FIVE STRING BANJO AMERICAN FOLK STYLE is a most successful attempt at basic analysis of traditional and contemporary banjo techniques and styles; the student who approaches it from this point of view will find it a richly-packed source of ideas. It is not an easy five-minute instructor; it makes demands on the player, but the eventual rewards for this method of study are great. For one last remark, don't re-

By Bess Hawes, in Sing Out magazine.

If you live near a large library you can find there dozens of books on the banjo, written forty to a hundred years ago. Most of them pay scant attention to folk styles of playing. If you are interested, here's the titles of some of them, with their Library of Congress numbers:

Sketches of Noted Banjo Players
  S. Stewart   ML 395   .S 85
Eno's Elementary And Advanced Technique -
  Paul Eno Mt 565 .E 59
Banjo With Full Instructions - John Picht
  Mt 568   .593
Banjo Lessons - composed and edited by
  F. J. Bacon   Mt 568   .S 578
Converse's Analytical Banjo Method -
  Mt 562   .C64

The Universal Banjo Method -
  Clarence L. Partee Mt-561 .P975
Practical Hints On Modern Banjo Playing -
  Clarence L. Partee   Mt-560   .P27
Christy's Minstrel's Complete Banjo Tutor -
  Mt 568   .R45
The Minstrel Banjoist - S. S. Stewart -
  Mt 562   .S87   M5
Lagatree's Banjo Tutor - Mt 568   .L26
C Notation Excelsior Method for the Banjo -
  G. L. Lansing   Mt-562 .L297
Phil Rice's Method For The Banjo -
  Mt 568   .R45
Pan-American School For The Banjo -
  W.B. Leonard Mt.568 .L 39
Sherwood's Imperial Diagram Method For
  The Banjo - Mt 562 .S 656
Tone And Technic - Edwin Pritchard
  MT 565 .P75
Crown Figure Method For The Banjo -
  C. Himmelman & Co. Mt 568 .C 78
Elias Howe's New Banjo Without A Master -
  Mt 568 .H71
The Perpetual Banjo School, No. 3,8,9, & 10-
  D. Mansfield Mt-561 .M392, .M454,
  .M606, .M607
Shay's Banjo School - William Shay
  Mt-562.S660
Banjo Method, Lessons 1,2,3,4 -
  Royal Music Co. Mt-562 .R88
The Eclipse Self-Instructor For Banjo -
  Paul De Ville Mt-568 .494
Dobson's New System For The Banjo -
  George C. Dobson Mt 568 .D 673
New School For the Banjo -
  George C. Dobson Mt 561 .D63

In England, similar banjo material is available from Clifford Essex Ltd., 8 New Compton St. London WC2.

GUS CANNON 1925? (S.CHARTERS PHOTO)

BOOKS OF SONGS TO SING

Literally hundreds of folk song collections are now available in Libraries. Some large cities have bookstores which specialize in them. Here we list just a few, with apologies to the many whose titles have had to be omitted.

A Treasury Of Folksong, Kolb, Bantam Books, 35¢. The cheapest but one of the best.

Various song 'kits' put out by the Cooperative Recreation Service, Deleware, Ohio, 25¢ each.

Lift Every Voice, and the People's Songbook, from Sing Out Magazine, 107 Lafayette St., NYC.

Traditional Tunes Of The Child Ballads, Bronson, Princeton University Press, ($$$ but worth 'em).

Folk Songs of North America, Alan Lomax, 623 pp., Doubleday NYC. Also earlier books by the Lomaxes: Cowboy Songs, American Ballad And Folk Songs, Our Singing Country and Best Loved American Folk Songs.

The American Songbag, Carl Sandburg, Harcourt Brace, NYC.

The Weaver's Songbook, Harpers, NYC. Also The Weavers Sing and The Caroler's Songbag, Folkways Music Pub. 10 Columbus Circle, NYC. Same publisher has 'Leadbelly', songs of the late Huddie Ledbetter, $2.00.

Folk Blues, edited by Jerry Silverman, MacMillan, NYC.

California To New York Island - songs of Woody Guthrie, pub. by Woody Guthrie Publications Inc. Suite 2017, 250 W. 57 NYC. Cecil Sharpe, Oxford University Press. Also from the same publisher, The Oxford Book Of Carols.

Woody Guthrie Songbook - E. P. Dutton.

Folk Songs Of Canada, Ed. by Edith Fowke, Waterloo Music Co. Waterloo, Canada.

Songs Of Work And Freedom, Fowke and Glazer, Roosevelt University, 430 S. Michigan Ave., Chicago, Ill.

The Shuttle And The Cage, and Personal Choice, two fine collections by Ewan MacColl, available in USA through Hargail Music Press, 28 W. 38th St., NYC.

The Abelard Folksong Book, by Norman Cazden, Abelard Shuman, NYC.

Folksongs And Footnotes, Theodore Bikel, Meridian Books.

American Folk Songs For Children, Animal Folk Songs and American Folk Songs For Christmas, all by Ruth Crawford Seeger, Doubleday, NYC.

Songs To Grow On, Beatrice Landeck, E. B. Marks, NYC.

Crown Publishers has the series of 'Treasuries' edited by Ben Botkin. Good also are the Treasury of Mexican Folklore and the Treasury of Jewish Folklore.

American Favorite Ballads, edited by Moe Asch, Irwin Silber and yours truly. 96 pp, paperback. Oak Pub. 33 W. 60 NYC.

Burl Ives Sea Songs, 131 pp. Ballantine Books.

Last but not least, anyone interested in folk music should subscribe to a little publication which every two months comes out with new and old songs, reviews of books and records, and articles of many kinds. Practically every good song I know has been printed there at some time or other. It is called SING OUT, 107 Lafayette St., NYC. One Year $3.00, two years $5.00 and worth it ten times over.

Homemade Banjo   Photo by John Cohen

APPENDIX 7

PHONOGRAPH RECORDS

If you can beg, borrow, or steal some of the following phonograph records, you'll best learn the style and sweep of the banjo. If the records are 78 rpm you can play them at 33 rpm and analyze what notes are being played. If they are already LP you could perhaps rerecord them on tape and play them back at a slower speed.

Some of the very best records of banjo playing are unfortunately now out of print. They were recorded for the major record companies for their "Country Music" catalogues in the 20's and 30's, and never re-issued. However, at the time of writing (1961) the following records can be ordered by mail.

The American Folklife Center, Library of Congress, Washington, D.C., issues on LP and 78 some of the very best examples of American folk music. Write for their catalogue (25¢). Although the sound quality is poor by today's standards, they are still my top choices. For Example:

> Pretty Polly, by Pete Steele (#L1 & #5 (78)
> Pay Day At Coal Creek, Pete Steele (#L2)
> Roll On The Ground, (#L2)
> Chilly Winds, by Wade Ward (#L2 & #9)
> Coal Creek March, Pete Steele (#L2 & #9)
> The Rambling Boy, Justus Begley (#L7 & #31)
> Sally Goodin, Justus Begley (#L9 & #41)
> Blue-Eyed Girl, Rufus Crisp (#L20 & #96)

The Folkways Recording Company, 632 Broadway, NYC, has reissued some of the old commercial recordings of Uncle Dave Macon and others and has also located and re-recorded some more old timers. Folkways also releases the banjo instructor LP which goes along with this book. They also have more recordings of me than anyone should bother listening to. I suggest you order their catalogue and look into some of the following: Anthology of American Folk Music, edited by Harry Smith; American Banjo, Scruggs Style; Mountain Music of Kentucky; also check records by performers such as Pete Steele, Stoneman Family, Bascom Lunsford, Roscoe Holcomb, Buell Kazee, Clarence Ashley, the New Lost City Ramblers, Peggy Seeger.

Folk-Lyric Recording Company, 3323 Morning Glory Ave., Baton Rouge, La., has a fine LP of banjo songs by my sister Peggy.

In England, look up Topic Records, 27 Nassington Rd., London NW2; the Brunswick re-issue of Cousin Emmy (#9258-9); other folk music records can be found at Collet's Record Shop, 70 New Oxford Street, London WC1. In Australia, look up Wattle Recordings.

Atlantic Records, 75 Rockefeller Plaza, NYC has a fine folk music series edited by Alan Lomax, including an LP "Blue Ridge Mountain Music" with banjoes.
Recordings of Earl Scruggs and other bluegrass musicians are listed on p. 45. Frailers on p. 37.

Capitol Records still releases Cliffie Stone's Square Dance LP, with Cliffie's father, Herman the Hermit, playing superb banjo on them.

Vanguard Records, 71 W. 23rd St., NYC 10001 has a good deal of banjo music in its series on the Newport Folk Festivals of 1959-60, and its numerous LPs of the Weavers. They expect soon to release records by Eric Darling, and by the Greenbriar Boys (bluegrass).

Prestige-International, 203 S. Washington Ave., Bergenfield, New Jersey, has LPs by Peggy Seeger.

Elektra Records, 1017 N. La Cienega Blvd., Los Angeles, Cal. 90069. has a large catalogue of folk music, some of it with banjo (Bob Gibson, Roger Sprung, Peggy Seeger, Eric Darling).

Most of the major companies issue recordings like a magazine prints issues - when they are sold out, they are not reprinted. Thus some of the best folk banjo playing has been issued and is no longer available on Decca, Victor, and Columbia. These companies, however, can supply good bluegrass records, since that is selling well nowadays. See page 45.

In listening to recordings you'll come across some songs that you want to learn. Remember, you yourself have to decide then to what extent you want to imitate them note for note, and to what extent you want to change them. There are dangers in either extreme.

The above is a very incomplete listing. If any readers feels I have missed reporting something really good, let me know, so I can include the information in a future edition.* Meanwhile, you can find listings of current folk music recordings in Sing Out Magazine, PO Box 5460 Bethlehem, PA 18015.

> Q. Kath.: Take thy lute, wench:
> My soul grows sad with
> troubles;
> Sing and disperse 'em,
> if thou canst.
> " King Henry VIII.,"
> Act III., Scene 1.

*Ha, ha.